From the Library of
David C. Morgan

Getting
Acquainted
with the
Bible

D0368291

Getting Acquainted with

The Bible

Herschel H. Hobbs

© Copyright 1991 Convention Press
All rights reserved

5132-75

This book is the text for Course Number 04-125
in the subject area "Bible Studies" in the Church
Study Course

Getting acquainted with the Bible
Dewey Decimal Classification: 220
Subject Heading: BIBLE

Printed in the United States of America

Sunday School Division
The Sunday School Board of the Southern
Baptist Convention
127 Ninth Ave., North
Nashville, Tennessee 37234

Scripture quotations marked (NKJV) are from
the Holy Bible, *New King James Version.* Copyright 1979, 1980, 1982 by Thomas Nelson, Inc.

Dedicated to

Bible Lovers and Readers Everywhere

—may you live it to God's glory.

Contents

Editor: *Louie L. Wilkinson*

Introduction

Many people take their Bibles for granted, and consequently neglect them. This little book serves a twofold purpose. It introduces you to a commentary on the Bible. And it is intended to show how the Bible came to be what it is. Obviously in so small a book various subjects must be treated briefly. But the author prays that it will be sufficient to help you to appreciate and use your Bible.

My first year out of high school I was gainfully employed. So for Christmas I gave my mother a large Bible. When she died, it was the only one of her possessions I requested for myself. When I turn its pages I can tell which were her favorite passages. This was evident from the body oil from her fingers which colored the margin of the pages.

May this little volume lead you to color many pages of your Bible. If so, its purpose will be accomplished.

Herschel H. Hobbs

The Bible:

A Unique Book

Chapter 1
The Bible: A Unique Book

The story is told of Sir Walter Scott when he was terminally ill. He asked a friend to read to him from the Book. Since he had a large library, the friend asked, "Which book?" Scott replied, "There is but one Book, the Bible."

"Bible" comes from the Greek word *biblos,* meaning "book." Another Greek word is also used. It is *biblia,* meaning "little books." The Book is composed of 66 little books, 39 in the Old Testament and 27 in the New Testament.

These little books were written over a period of about fifteen hundred years in places all the way from Babylon to Rome. There were approximately 45 different authors ranging all the way from kings to poets, to prophets, to a physician, to farmers and shepherds, to fishermen, to a tax collector, to apostles, to a pastor and other spiritual leaders. Not a one knew that he was writing what would become a part of the Holy Bible.

Yet when gathered together into the canon of Scripture, they tell a complete story. If someone should read the New Testament without a knowledge of the Old Testament, he would ask, "What came before this?" If one should read the Old Testament without a knowledge of the New, he would ask, "Where is the rest of the story?" When properly understood no book contradicts the others. No book adds to previously written truth except to enlarge upon it or interpret it.

These things cannot be said about any other set of books. The only reasonable explanation of this is that they have a common author—God through His Holy Spirit.

To understand this truth calls for the examination of three other truths: revelation, inspiration, and illumination! For all three are involved in the substance, recording, and interpretation of the Bible.

Revelation

This word might well be spelled re-veal-a-tion. Strictly it means an unveiling. The last book in the Bible (Revelation) is called "Revelation" from the word *apokalupsis*, meaning unveiling. "God is love" (1 John 4:8). And love reveals itself. Thus God is not discovered through human wisdom or reason. "For after that in the wisdom of God the world by wisdom knew not [did not come to know] God" (1 Cor. 1:21). Paul used the word "mystery" to denote that which man cannot achieve through human reason but which must be received through divine revelation.

Not only does God reveal Himself, but man is capable of receiving that revelation. God created man in His image and likeness (Gen. 1:26-27). The Supreme Person created the finite person. "Image" and "likeness" does not refer to the physical but to the spiritual nature.

We speak of the competency of the soul in religion. This does not refer to human self-sufficiency, but to man's ability as a person to have direct dealing with God without the need for any human mediator or institution. Neither

does it mean that one can believe just anythi
and call himself a Christian—Baptist, Methoι
or whatever. It means that as a person man h
the right of choice. But he is responsible to G
for his choices.

The author of Hebrews says that God has revealed Himself at many times and in many way
(1:1a). For instance, God reveals Himself in his
creation. In showing that anyone who rejects
God is without excuse, Paul says, "Because that
which may be known of God is manifest in [to]
them; for God hath shewed it unto them. For the
invisible things of him from the creation of
the world are clearly seen, being understood by
the things that are made, even his eternal power
and Godhead [Godhood]; so that they are without excuse" (Rom. 1:19-20). Furthermore, David
in Psalm 19:1-3 declared, "The heavens declare
the glory of God; and the firmament sheweth his
handywork. Day unto day uttereth speech, and
night unto night sheweth knowledge. There is
no speech nor language, where their voice is not
heard."

The Bible dismisses the atheist with two
verses. "The fool hath said in his heart, There is
no God" (Pss. 14:1; 53:1). A "fool" is an unthink-
ing person who does not reason through a
matter to its logical conclusion. But note that he
does not say it in his mind but in his heart, the
seat of the will or wish. In his mind he knows
that there is a God. In his heart he *wishes* there
were no God to whom he is responsible.

Anyone with an unprejudiced mind can see
God's revelation in towering mountains, a sun-

rise or a sunset, the beauty of a flower, and the symmetry of a snowflake. When the first Russian cosmonauts returned from outer space they said, "We did not see God anywhere." The American astronauts returned, saying, "We saw God everywhere."

Also God reveals Himself in the human *conscience.* In Romans 2 Paul compares Jew and Gentile in their knowledge of God. Of the Gentiles (pagans) he says, "For when the Gentiles, which have not the [written] law, do by nature the things contained in the law, these, having not the law, are a law unto themselves: Which shew the work of the law written in their hearts, their conscience also bearing witness, and their thoughts the mean while accusing or else excusing one another" (2:14-15). Even the pagan knows better than he does.

Helen Keller was born blind, deaf, and mute. Her companion and teacher devised a method of communicating with her by tapping in her hand. When she first learned about God, Miss Keller has been quoted as saying, "I knew Him! I knew Him! I didn't know His name, but I knew Him!"

God reveals Himself in His *mighty acts* in history. His redemption of Israel from Egyptian bondage and settlement in Canaan are repeatedly cited as the nucleus of Israel's faith in God (cf. Ex. 19:4; Joshua 24:2-18). We will discuss this phase of God's revelation more fully in Chapter 2.

Likewise, God reveals Himself through His *written Word.* Of course, this revelation is clearer than the ones mentioned above. Theologians speak of progressive revelation. This does not mean that God began by revealing Himself crudely and leaned how to do so better as He went along. It means that He revealed Himself progressively as man was able to receive and comprehend His revelation.

Had Einstein taught a child mathematics, he would not have started with his theory of relativity. He would have started with one plus one equals two—not because that was all the mathematics he knew, but because that was all the child could absorb at the time.

Thus we have a clearer picture of God in John than in Genesis. But He is the same God in both. God's redemptive purpose runs throughout the Bible. But it is seen more completely in the New Testament than in the Old Testament.

God's full revelation is seen in His *living Word*. Jesus Christ (Heb. 1:1-3). God is One (Deut. 6:4). But He reveals Himself to us as Father, Son, and Holy Spirit. This threefold revelation is one of relationships. It is a mystery beyond our comprehension. But if you remove the mystery from the Judeo-Christian faith, you have only a moral philosophy.

Many efforts have been made to explain the threefold nature of God. For instance, some liken it to water, steam, and ice—the same substance but in three different appearances and functions.

However, God is the infinite Person, and He created man as a finite person. So any figure of this relationship must involve persons, not things.

No earthly illustration can suffice. But for me the nearest I have come in depicting the triune God is a threefold relationship I bore to my wife. I was her pastor, her husband, and the father of her child. I am not three people, but one, bearing three distinct relationships to her. In Romans 8:9, Paul calls the Holy Spirit the Spirit of God and the Spirit of Christ.

All three Persons of the Godhead were involved in both creation (Gen. 1:1-2; John 1:3) and redemption. As for the latter, God the Father *proposed* redemption; God the Son *provided* redemption; God the Holy Spirit *propagates* redemption.

Jesus said, "He that hath seen me hath seen the Father" (John 14:9), and "I and my Father are one" (John 10:30). Paul said, "God was in Christ, reconciling the world unto himself" (2 Cor. 5:19).

One of the richest passages in the Bible is John's introduction of his Gospel (John 1:1-18). It shows how the eternal God has revealed Himself in Jesus Christ. Through the centuries God through the prophets at "various times and in different ways spoke . . . has in these last days [His full, final revelation] spoken to us by His Son" or one bearing the relationship of Son (Heb. 1:1-2, NKJV).

In the light of "spoke" it is significant that John introduces Christ as the "Word." This translates *logos*, the open, spoken manifestation of the speaker (John 1:1,14; 1 John 1:1). In light of "In the beginning" (Gen. 1:1; John 1:1), it is of interest to note that in Genesis 1 each new phase of God's creative work is introduced by "and God said." Here is His open, spoken manifestation—His Word. John 1:3 pictures the Word or Christ as the intermediate Agent in the creative act.

However, the most significant thing in this passage is seen in verses 1 and 14. Literally, "In the beginning always was the Word [Christ], and the Word always was equal with God, and the Word always was God himself . . . And the Word became flesh and dwelt among us . . . full of grace and truth."

"Always was" translates the verb "to be" (*eimi*), expressing essential, and in this case, eternal being. In verse 14 "became" renders the verb "to become (*ginomai*). The eternal Christ became something He had never been before—a flesh and blood man—that He might reveal God as redeeming love. When God revealed His law He did so through a man—Moses. When He revealed His grace He became a man—Jesus of Nazareth. We say that Jesus of Nazareth was God, and so He was and is. But a more thrilling thing is that God became Jesus of Nazareth—for us.

John adds in verse 18 that "No one has seen [with the natural eyes] God at any time. The only begotten Son . . . has declared Him" (NKJV). "Declared" renders a verb transliterated into English as "exegeted." It means to draw out of a word or passage of Scripture its true meaning. So Jesus Christ has "exegeted" God the Father so that we see Him as He is. Thus Jesus says that in seeing Him we see the Father. What Jesus did/does we see God doing. This is why the article on "The

Scriptures" in *The Baptist Faith and Message*
closes with the words "The criterion by which
the Bible is to be interpreted is Jesus Christ."

Inspiration

Inspiration denotes the means by which God's
revelation was recorded in what we call the Bible.
"Inspire" means to breathe in. In both Hebrew
and Greek, the languages of the Old and New
Testaments respectively, the words for spirit or
Spirit also mean wind or breath. So inspiration
in terms of the Scriptures is a work of God
through the Holy Spirit.

In 2 Peter 1:20-21 the apostle says, "No prophecy of the scripture is of any private interpretation" (v. 20). Unfortunately, "interpretation" is
not a good translation. This reads as if only certain people are qualified to interpret the Bible. It
should read "of private origin." No one sets out
on his own to be a prophet. Or, as A. T.
Robertson used to say, that no prophet is a "self-
starter." It does not come through man's will but
through God's will. "Holy men of God spake as
they were moved by the Holy Ghost [Spirit]"
(v. 21). "Moved" translates a verb meaning "to
bear" as a ship carries its cargo. This does not
mean that the speakers and writers were autom-
atons, but that they were "in the Spirit" (Rev.
1:10) as they spoke or wrote.

In 2 Timothy 3:16 Paul says, "All scripture is
given by inspiration of God." Literally, "All
scripture is God-breathed." Some interpreters
hold that "all scripture" is "God-breathed", but
they do not regard parts of the Bible as Scrip-

ture. Paul did not hold to this view. In the original Greek text "all" is without the definite article. It should read that "every single part of the whole of scripture is God-breathed." And since God is a God of truth, He does not breathe error. (See Chapter 3 for further treatment of this.)

There are two principal theories as to the method by which the Holy Spirit inspired the writers of Scripture. One is called the *verbal plenary theory.* The other is called the *dynamic theory.*

The verbal plenary theory holds that the Holy Spirit inspired every word in the Bible. Some call this the *dictation* theory, or that the Holy Spirit dictated the words and the writers merely recorded them.

One problem which I find with this position is found where different Gospel writers, reporting the same event, use different words. For instance, Matthew 13:24 uses "kingdom of heaven." Mark 4:11 and Luke 8:10 use "kingdom of God." Also when Jesus spoke of a camel going through the eye of a needle, Matthew and Mark use the word for a sewing needle. Luke, a physician, uses the word for a surgical needle. Each used the word with which he was most familiar (Matt. 19:24; Mark 10:25; Luke 18:25). Of course, these are minor matters. But they do warn against dogmatism at this point.

The *dynamic theory* holds that the Holy Spirit inspired the writers, guided them in their work, guarded them from error, but left each free to choose his words and to inject his own personality into his writings. However, it is not the method of inspiration used but the *product* which is of primary importance. Both schools of thought hold that the product is the divinely inspired Word of God!

The different biblical writers obtained material from different sources. This is another reason why I lean toward the dynamic theory of inspiration. The use of different sources should not disturb one's faith in divine inspiration. The Holy Spirit guided them in finding and using these sources.

A good example of this is Luke's gospel. In Luke 1:1-4, Luke tells of his use of oral and written sources for his Gospel. The verb tenses in this passage indicate that he is not telling what he planned to do, but what he had done. Apparently Luke wrote these words after finishing the body of his Gospel.

It was probably during Paul's two-year imprisonment in Caesarea that Luke used this time to search out this material. Many who had been with Jesus had stories to tell about His ministry. Some had written them down. As a physician Luke had a scientific mind. He knew how to do research, to evaluate evidence, and to draw conclusions. And having done so he wrote them down in chronological order.

It is even possible that Luke talked with Mary herself. To a physician more than to anyone else she would talk about the conception and birth of Jesus. In any case Luke was so convinced about this that he wrote the most complete story of Jesus' birth. The same is true of His resurrection. And this in spite of the fact that his technical training as a physician would prejudice him against both.

Matthew, Mark, and Luke are called the Synoptic Gospels. This means that they present the life of Jesus from a similar point of view. And it is generally agreed that Mark was the first Gospel to be written. Suggested dates for Mark range from A.D. 50 to A.D. 65. A date in the first half of the 50's seems most likely. Dates for Matthew and Luke range from the late 50's into the 80's. Matthew probably wrote in the late 50's. Assuming that Luke gathered his material during Paul's Caesarean imprisonment, he could have written late in the Caesarean or early in Paul's Roman imprisonment. This would place it sometime in A.D. 60-61.

Significant is the use of Mark in Matthew and Luke. Generally they follow Mark's framework and often use Mark's exact words. At times either will depart from it. But where one veers from it the other usually stays with it.

More than half of Mark's language can be seen in both Matthew and Luke.

However, both Matthew and Luke contain material not found in Mark. This is referred to as Q. from *quelle*, the German word for "source." At the same time each of these Gospels has material peculiar to itself. For instance, Matthew 2 is peculiar to that Gospel. It relates the virgin birth of Jesus from the standpoint of Joseph, though Matthew is careful to show that Joseph was not Jesus' real father. Only here do we have the story of the magi and Herod's effort to kill Jesus in His infancy. On the other hand, only Luke relates the birth of John the Baptist. This Gospel alone tells of Gabriel's visit to Mary and subsequent events leading to Jesus' birth in Bethlehem and accompanying events, including the shepherds, angelic chorus, and the presentation of the infant Jesus in the Temple. Luke's emphasis upon music in his birth narrative led someone to suggest that he may have been a musician.

Even though both Matthew and Luke contain the Sermon on the Mount, Matthew contains much material not found in Luke's account. Also Luke contains material peculiar to itself. This is especially true of Luke 9:51—18:14. It reports a Judean ministry found in none of the other Gospels. However, it contains teachings of Jesus which Matthew reports in His Galilean ministry. But there is no reason why He would not use them also in Judea where the audience was different from the one in Galilee.

The Gospel of John, on the other hand, is unique in its approach to the life of Jesus. An old tradition says that Mary and the Apostle lived in Jerusalem until shortly before A.D. 70 and then moved to Ephesus. Writing sometime between A.D. 80-90, long after the Synoptic Gospels, John supplements the account of the synoptic writers. He parallels them only in the feeding of the five thousand (John 6) and in his coverage of the last week of Jesus' life. Even in the parallels he gives details not found in the others. He relates the feeding of the multitudes only to show the immediate cause for the collapse of Jesus' Galilean ministry. Never thereafter did the crowds follow Jesus in Galilee.

John 2:1—4:42 A. T. Robertson calls "A Year of Obscurity." This records events prior to the beginning of Jesus' Galilean ministry. But 4:43-54 shows that John is aware of this ministry.

The phrases "after this" and "after these things" (cf. John 5:1; 6:1; 7:1) seem to be a formula by which John indicates that he is inserting into the Synoptic account bodies of material not found in the other three Gospels. John 7—10 fits into Luke 9:51—18:14 to present a ministry in Jerusalem and Judea which is not recorded in Matthew and Mark. John 14—17 is peculiar to John's Gospel.

If we had only the Synoptic Gospels, it would appear that the first visit to Jerusalem in His public ministry Jesus was crucified. But John records three visits to Jerusalem prior to the final one (John 2:13; 5:1; 10:22). In each of these we see a growing hostility toward Jesus on the part of the Jewish leaders. These not only explain their opposition to Jesus in Galilee, but they set the stage for the final climax at Calvary. Though John 11 records a visit of Jesus to Bethany near Jerusalem, in the raising of Lazarus from the dead Jesus threw down the gauntlet to the Sanhedrin. This led to that body's firm resolve to kill Jesus. Truly the Gospel account would be incomplete without the Gospel of John.

Illumination

Illumination is the work of the Holy Spirit whereby He enables us to recall and to understand the Scriptures. For instance, though Jesus, the Master Teacher, had repeatedly taught the apostles about His coming death, they did not fully understand it until after the Holy Spirit came upon them at Pentecost. And it is through both inspiration and illumination by the Holy Spirit that we can understand the writing of the New Testament. (The same is true of the Old Testament. But it is more clearly seen in the New Testament. Space considerations lead us to concentrate on the latter.)

However, one general word needs to be said. The ancient Greeks produced some of the greatest minds the world has ever seen. Someone humorously remarked that the Greeks stole all of our original ideas five hundred years before Jesus was born. Yet their philosophical writings neither probed to the deepest depths of man's spiritual needs nor soared to the heights of divine glory as do the Scriptures. Comparing Greek philosophical wisdom to divine wisdom, Paul said, "Where is the wise? Where is the scribe? Where is the disputer of this age? Has not God made foolish the wisdom of this world? For since, in the wisdom of God, the world through wisdom did not know [come to know] God, it pleased God through the foolishness of the message preached to save those who believe" (1 Cor. 1:20-21, NKJV). One Greek philosopher said that he did not know how God would save man. It might be through a God or God-man. And that is as near to divine inspiration as Greek philosophy ever came.

On the night before His death Jesus promised His apostles that He would pray that the Father would send the Comforter whom He identified as the Holy Spirit of truth. And when He comes, "he shall teach you all things, and bring all things to your remembrance, whatsoever I have said unto you" (John 14:26). Also, "he will guide you into all truth" (John 16:13). He spoke of spiritual truth, not scientific truth or otherwise. This the Spirit did/does through illumination. And He "will shew you things to come" (v. 13). We see the fulfillment of these promises in the remainder of the New Testament.

Jesus said of the Spirit. "He shall glorify me" (John 16:14). The Spirit does not point to Himself but to Christ. It is thus that the New Testament writers were able to interpret God's revelation in Jesus Christ, to apply His teachings and redemptive work to our needs, and to point to the glory and ultimate victory of Christ.

The Holy Spirit still illuminates our minds and hearts so that we may understand and apply God's word to our lives. Someone said, "I know that the Bible is a divine book, for it speaks to me at a depth which no other book does."

A. T. Robertson was perhaps the leading New Testament scholar of his generation. In his senior Greek class on a Monday afternoon in September, 1934, I sat within ten feet of him when a stroke came on him that killed him an hour and a half later. On the previous Friday he gave us what was possibly his greatest testimony concerning the New Testament. Said he, "For over fifty years I have been studying, writing, teaching, and preaching the New Testament. But I never read my Greek New Testament without finding something I never saw before." That is illumination!

I could not hold a light for him as he read the New Testament. But after sixty years I can say the same thing.

You can still learn all there is to know about other books. But not about the Bible. Truly it is an inexhaustible spring from which to drink. And it will never run dry! The Bible is a unique book indeed!

The Bible

and
History

Chapter 2
The Bible and History

The Bible was not written in heaven, printed on rice paper, bound in leather bearing in gold letters the imprint "Holy Bible," and thrown down to earth. It was wrought out in the arena of history. Biblical writings spoke God's message to those living in a definite historical setting. At the same time they speak to us in our historical environments. The Bible sets forth eternal truth which was/is timely. That truth is also timeless in nature. Men may live in different historical settings. But their inner spiritual needs are ever the same. And truth which God spoke to Abraham applies to our needs in similar circumstances.

Since the Bible tells of real people living under specific historical conditions, a knowledge of the history involved enables us better to understand the message of the Bible.

Definition of History

"History" comes from the Greek word *historia*, meaning *inquiry*. It is the treating of conditions and events in given times in the past which affected nations and peoples. It is more than merely recording events. It seeks to interpret them on a broad scale as to their effect upon the whole spectrum of human events.

So history is not merely the recording of events as in a log or massive diary. Historians seek to interpret these in order to ascertain the effect of events upon mankind. For the most part secular historians study the effect of geography, political forces, intellectual thought, and social orders upon the various people involved. Careful and copious treatment is given to the surface events of history. But, Jesus Christ was no mere "surface" event. He has affected the history of the world as has no other person who ever lived. Yet if secular historians treat Him at all He is given scant treatment.

The Bible is not a textbook on history. Yet its story fits into the framework of recorded history. Furthermore, it records history not found in any other book. Yet when properly understood it fits into the pattern of the records of secular historiographers.

Divine Philosophy of History

In his sermon on Mars Hill in Athens, Paul sets forth the divine philosophy of history.

God "giveth to all life, and breath, and all things; and hath made of [ex, out of] one . . . all nations [ethnos, ethnic groups] of men for to dwell on all the face of the earth, and hath determined the times before appointed, and the bounds of their habitation; That they should seek the Lord, if haply they might feel after him, and find him, though he be not far from every one of us: For in him we live, and move, and have our being; as certain also of your own poets have said, For we are also his offspring" (Acts 17:25-28).

Note that "blood" is not in the oldest and best manuscripts. The reference is to Adam as the federal head of the race. No nation emerges from the womb of time as a surprise to God. He has determined beforehand the time of their rising and the boundaries of their habitation. And no nation falls but that He takes note of it.

A. T. Robertson says, "Nations rise and fall, but it is not blind chance or hard fate. Thus there is an interplay between God's will and man's activities, difficult as it is for us to see with our shortened vision."[1]

It is God's will that all nations seek Him, that they find and fill their role in His plan and purpose. Sadly the highway of history is littered with the debris of fallen nations which either did not recognize God or else departed from Him.

That such are without excuse is evident in the fact that "he be not far from every one of us" (v. 27). Furthermore, Paul quotes from pagan poets to prove a Christian truth.

T. C. Smith points out that *In him we live, and move, and have our being* "is possibly a modification of part of a poem by Epimenides, a sage of Greece in the sixth century B.C." "'For we are indeed his offspring' comes from Aratus (*Phaenomena*, line 5), the poet from Tarsus in the fourth century B.C. who greatly influenced Stoic thought."[2]

Defenders of evolution for many years held that man began by worshiping many gods and some gradually came to worship one god or God. This idea, of course, denied Genesis 1-2 and Romans 1. The sciences of anthropology and archaeology contain evidence that man began by worshiping one God and gradually descended to the worship of numerous gods. Of course, this concurs with the biblical account.

What it all boils down to is that the God who called out Israel and who sent His only Son to be Savior of the world is the God of history. He is not responsible for the evil deeds of men and/or nations, but they are responsible to Him. He judges nations within the context of history. While individuals face the timely consequences of their evil deeds, the Bible points to the final judgment at the end of the age (Rev. 20). Furthermore, it points to a redeemed and subdued cosmic order in which "God may be all in all" (1 Cor. 15:25-28).

In the meantime God works in all things within the context of history "for good to them that love God, to them who are the called according to his purpose" (Rom. 8:28). Within the hue and cry, "bubble bubble, toil and trouble" of men and nations God is overruling the evil and guiding events toward the accomplishment of His will and redemptive purpose.

History Within History

While it is true that a knowledge of ancient history contributes to our understanding of the Bible, it is also true that the Bible does not contain a complete account of ancient history. The Bible touches upon only those portions of history which are directly related to the purpose of the Bible. And in that sense the Bible sheds light upon a fuller understanding of secular history.

Thus there is a *history within history*. We may call it *holy history,* or *redemptive history.* For whereas secular historians relate the surface facts of the movements of history, there is an undercurrent which relates the surface events to God's purpose in history. Several examples may be cited in this regard.

For instance, let us look at the land of *Canaan* or Palestine. While other nations figure in the biblical account, the focal geographical point in the Bible is Canaan. Strictly speaking it is a strip of land about forty-five miles wide and seventy-five miles long. To secular historians who write from the standpoint of the political centers of ancient empires, it was an area out on the edge of those empires which bore little importance to them.

Someone asked a question. If God was going to redeem the world, why did He have His Son to live and die in a small area on the backside of the world? Such a question reveals a lack of understanding of the ancient world. For in fact this little strip of land was at the center of the ancient world.

Canaan was a land bridge between a desert on the east and the Mediterranean Sea on the west. "Mediterranean" means "middle of the world." This land bridge connected the three known continents of the ancient world—Africa, Asia, and Europe. The traffic of these three continents moved through this focal point of the ancient world. International highways converged upon it. Over them moved the caravans of commerce; armies moved back and forth over them. Because of Canaan's strategic location, it became a political football between mighty empires contending for world supremacy. Some of the most strategic battles of the ancient world were fought in or near it. These are the things of which secular historians write.

But the Bible relates history within history. The outworking of God's eternal redemptive purpose in history begins with Abraham. To him and his seed God promised Canaan as a homeland. For it was through his descendant Israel that He proposed to carry forward that purpose. Located in the heart of the ancient world, it was to be the hub from which the priest-nation Israel was to bring pagan nations to worship and serve God. Also from that land almost two thousand years later Christians were to move in evangelizing their world.

Again, even if a historian deemed the exodus epic worthy of note, he probably would see it only as the migration of a large body of people who ultimately settled in Canaan. But the sacred historian recorded it as God's redemption of His people from Egyptian bondage, that they might become a covenant nation to be used in bringing pagan nations to God.

Historians recording the history of Assyria and Babylon might give brief notice to their respective victories over Israel and Judah, but only as having military and political significance. But the sacred historians give these occasions as God's discipline of faithless nations. The Bible makes no mention of the ultimate fate of the exiles in Assyria. Amos 9:8 calls it a "sinful" or "unlawful" kingdom. But it does record the return to Judah of a remnant of the exiles in Babylon.

Historians record the conquest of the Persian empire by Alexander the Great, including Palestine. In doing so, Alexander spread Greek culture over the ancient world. One result was that by the time of Jesus, Greek was practically a universal language. And while the Bible does not mention it in specific terms, this universal language made possible the rapid spread of the gospel and the writing of the New Testament in a language in wide use in the first century A.D. Looking back, we can see the hand of God amid man's atrocities of war making possible the above-mentioned work. Alexander the Great had no idea he was an instrument in God's hand to produce this result.

Likewise, historians record Rome's conquests. A by-product of these was the *Pax Romana* (Roman Peace of the sword), the establishing of sea lanes, and the building of roads which made possible rapid and safe travel for the evangels of grace which resulted in the rapid spread of the gospel.

So whether written or implied, we can see the hand of God at work within the context of secular history, preparing the way for "the fulness of the time" (Gal. 4:4). It was a time when the clouds of despair hovered over the Roman world. Pagan gods had proved to be empty vagaries. Turning to their rulers for hope, the people found them to be demons. Because of its monotheism and high moral standards, some Gentiles turned to Judaism. Others turned to the mystery religions that flooded the Empire—mixtures of oriental mysticism, Greek philosophy, and tinges of Hebrew theology—but they offered no soul-satisfying hope.

It was then that the Sun of righteousness

broke through the smog as the Light of the world. The Lily of the valley blossomed in all His glory, offering man beauty for ashes, and the eternal God became Jesus of Nazareth revealing God fully and finally as the God of redeeming love, grace, and truth.

True, in all this unfolding of history God's people suffered at the hands of oppressive nations. But less than three hundred years after Calvary and the empty tomb, the Roman emperor Constantine saw in Christianity the one cohesive force that could hold together in his crumbling empire.

Now at most points in time the faithful did not immediately see God's hand at work. But from our perspective through the pages of Holy Writ, we can see it. Like our forebears we may not readily see God's hand in current events. But it is there. Jesus said literally, "My Father keeps on working until now, and I myself keep on working" (John 5:17). And in that truth we find encouragement and peace.

Key to History

To-morrow, and to-morrow, and to-morrow
Creeps in this petty pace from day to day,
To the last syllable of recorded time;
And all our yesterdays have lighted fools
The way to dusty death. Out, out, brief candle!
Life's but a walking shadow, a poor player
That struts and frets his hour upon the stage
And then is heard no more: it is a tale
Told by an idiot, full of sound and fury,
Signifying nothing.
                                        —Shakespeare, *Macbeth*

Was Shakespeare right? When viewed in brief segments it would seem so. But is it? If history is not governed by chance, there must be a purpose, a goal which binds it together and gives it meaning. Frankly, I do not find it so in secular history. And this is not the biased opinion of one who loves history but is sadly lacking in training in historiography. But I quote Will and Ariel Durant who are historiographers.

"As his studies come to a close the historian faces the challenge: Of what use have his studies been? Have you found in your work only the amusement of recounting the rise and fall of nations and ideas, and retelling 'sad stories of the death of kings'? Have you learned more about human nature than the man in the street can learn without so much as opening a book? Have you derived from history any illumination of our present condition, any guidance for our judgments and policies, any guard against the rebuffs of surprise or the vicissitudes of change? Have you found such regularities in the sequence of past events that you can predict the future actions of mankind or the fate of states? Is it possible that, after all, 'history has no sense,' that it teaches us nothing, and that the immense past was only the weary rehearsal of the mistakes that the future is destined to make on a larger stage and scale?"[3] They confess that at times they feel so.

In order to find the one thing which binds the whole of history together, we must look to *holy history.* For, as previously stated, God is the God of history.

The book of Revelation is set in the context of Roman persecution of Christians. The Roman emperor Domitian (A.D. 81-96) demanded that all his subjects worship him as a god. Christians refused to do so and endured severe persecution, especially in the Roman province of Asia. Many paid with their lives; others endured suffering of various kinds. The Apostle John was in exile on the island of Patmos when he received the Revelation. Its overriding theme is the victory of Christ over all His foes. Edward A. McDowell calls Revelation the drama of the sovereignty of God.[4] After an introductory chapter and the letters to the seven churches of Asia (ch. 2—3), we have the first scene in the *drama* (Rev. 4—5).

In the midst of their sufferings the Christians evidently were asking questions. What is the meaning of all this? Has God been dethroned by Satan? Does God know what is happening to us? If He knows, does He not care? Worse still, does He know and care but is powerless to act on our behalf?

In this opening scene John was told not to *look about himself* at what was happening on earth. *Look up!* And see what is happening in heaven. The door to heaven was opened to give him a complete view. "And, behold, a throne was set in heaven, and one sat on the throne" (Rev. 4:2). The tense of "was set" means there had never been a time when that throne was not there. And its occupant was God. "And there was a rainbow round about [in a circle] the throne" (v. 3). This symbolized God's care for His people. And the hosts in heaven, redeemed people and natural order, were praising God for His creative work (vv. 4-11).

In God's right hand was a scroll (5:1). So great were its contents that they were written on both sides of the scroll. It was sealed with seven seals, completely sealed. And a voice was heard in heaven asking, "Who is worthy to open the book [scroll], and to loose the seals thereof?" (v. 2). To seal is to conceal; to unseal is to reveal. But no man in heaven, in earth, or under the earth was worthy to unseal the scroll (v. 4). Because of this, John wept. But an elder told him to stop weeping.

"Behold, the Lion of the tribe of Juda, the Root of David, hath prevailed to open the book, and to loose the seven seals thereof" (v. 5). "Prevailed" suggests the crucified and risen Christ who had thus proved God's sovereignty over the universe.

John looked up. But instead of a lion, he saw a "Lamb as it had been slain." He came and took the scroll. With this the redeemed, natural and spiritual orders, together with myriads of angels, began to praise the Lamb for His redemptive work.

Thus it was/is that no matter what may be happening on earth, in heaven God the Father is still on His throne and is being praised for His creative work. And God the Son is being praised for His redemptive work.

At this point let us examine the scroll and the unsealing of it. Many suggestions have been made as to the identity of this scroll. I see it as the scroll of history. Its meaning is to be seen in "no mere man—no saint in heaven, no man living on earth, no lost soul in hell—could [can] reveal the meaning of history. Historians endeavor to interpret history in terms of those who participate in it. They deal with persons and events. But this is to touch only the surface. They do not begin to get down to the true meaning of history."[5]

Only through God's redemptive purpose in Christ do we find the basic meaning of history. This purpose runs throughout the Bible so that we can understand the Bible only in light of this redemptive purpose.

We began this chapter by noting that to understand the Bible it must be interpreted in light of its historical context. And this is true. But as paradoxical as it may seem, it is equally true that we cannot understand history apart from the Bible. This gives credence to the words of one who said that no person can be said to be truly educated who does not know God's message in His recorded word, the Bible.

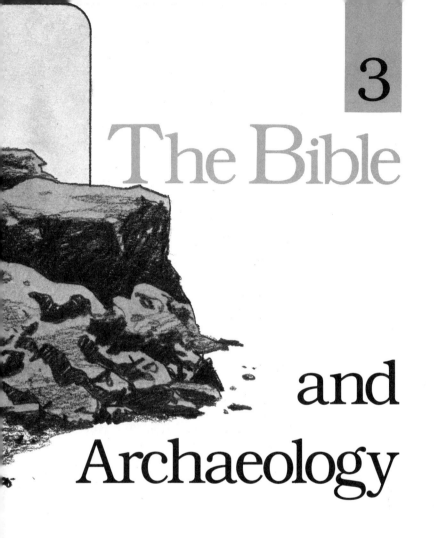

3

The Bible

and

Archaeology

Chapter 3
The Bible and Archaeology

When Jesus made His "Royal Entry" into Jerusalem on Sunday before His crucifixion, the people hailed Him with messianic cries (Matt. 21:1-11, 14-17; Mark 11:1-11; Luke 19:29-44; John 12:12-19), "Some of the Pharisees . . . said unto him, Master [teacher], rebuke thy disciples [pupils]" (Luke 19:39). Jesus said, "I tell you that, if these should hold their peace, the stones would immediately cry out" (Luke 19:40).

This is not necessarily a prophecy of Jesus concerning the modern science of archaeology. But it could well be seen as such. The fact is that archaeology has played a vital role in the study of the Bible. M. G. Kyle says, "Archaeology furnishes the true historical setting of Scripture."[1]

Definition of Archaeology
"Archaeology" (also spelled "archeology") comes from two Greek words (*archaios*, "ancient" and *logia*, "discourse"). The English word means the science of antiquities or of old things.

Of course, this science is related to the study of past civilizations, biblical and otherwise. But our present interest centers in its contributions to our understanding of the Bible.

Throughout the Middle East, especially in Palestine, one finds numerous "digs" in which archaeologists delve into the secrets of antiquity. Usually these "digs" are found at *Tees*, the Arabic word for mounds or hills. When ancient cities or towns were destroyed, rebuilders simply leveled the surface and built another over the previous ruins. Thus the deeper archeologists dig, the more ancient is the civilization. The science of archaeology is able to date various layers by the pottery and other artifacts uncovered. These, including the ruins of various constructions, enable them to determine the life and culture of various eras.

Several years ago an archaeologist friend and I led a custom-made tour of Palestine, Greece, Cyprus, and Turkey. Through his influence we were able to vist some of these "digs." Among other things we learned the care exercised to preserve every little piece of evidence. At the mound of Beersheba I watched one person excavating one clay pot intact. He even used a camel's hair brush to remove dust from the pot. We visited Herodium, the burial place of Herod the Great. Tiled floors and mural paintings were remarkably preserved. We even saw the method by which they controlled the temperature in the building by circulating hot water in winter and cold water in summer. These are only simple illustrations of how archaeology has enabled us to understand Bible times. Later in this chapter we will deal with more specific examples of how archaeology has thrown light on problems related to the authenticity of the Bible.

Jack Finegan makes the following summary statement. "The account which can now be given of the rise of civilization in the Middle East, of the development of art, and of the formulation of ethical, philosophical, and religious ideas is of fascinating interest in itself . . . To see that world come vividly and startlingly alive is to find biblical and early Christian history invested with a fresh sense of reality and interest. There are, moreover, many points at which biblical records and archeological discoveries are in direct contact, and increasingly in the later centuries there are many archeological remains which are primary historical monuments of Judasim and Christianity. A knowledge of these facts is now indispensable to all serious study of the Bible, and the proper utilization of the abundant new archeological materials may even be said to constitute one of the most important tasks in this study."[2]

Biblical Criticism

In everyday English, *criticism* means fault finding, but in Bible study, *criticism* refers to careful, exacting study. It is the careful gathering of evidence that sheds light on the meaning of Scripture. This term refers to two principle methods of Bible study. These methods are called *Lower* or *Textual Criticism* and *Higher Criticism*. The purpose of this book does not call for an exhaustive treatment of these. But a brief word about them shows their relation to archaeology.

James Orr says, "'Lower criticism' deals strictly with the *text* of Scripture, endeavoring to ascertain what the real text of each book was as it came from the hands of the author."[3]

Orr also defines "Higher Criticism." It "concerns itself with the resultant problems of age, authorship, sources, simple or composite character, historical worth, relation to period of origin, etc. The former—'textual criticism'—has a well-defined field in which it is possible to apply exact canons of judgment: the latter— 'higher criticism'—while invaluable as an aid in the domain of biblical introduction (date, authorship, genuineness, contents, destination, etc.), manifestly tends to widen out illimitably into regions where exact science cannot follow it, where, often, the critic's imagination is his only law."[4] This tends to make "Higher Criticism" a field of controversy.

Archaeology has played a significant role in both forms of criticism. It has provided manuscripts and other materials which enable Lower Criticism to do its work. Also it has served as a corrective measure with respect to what many call erroneous conclusions of many engaged in Higher Criticism. The remainder of this chapter will deal with such. For one thing, archaeology has shown that events and customs in Genesis (Abraham's life) reflect the historical setting found in Genesis. In light of what archaeology has already done, it is my opinion that it will have much more to say in the future.

Obviously in so brief a space we can only sketch a few of the more significant discoveries as they relate to the Bible. These are sufficient to show the tremendous contribution that archeology has made to the authenticity and the understanding of the Scriptures. The story reads like a romance and a detective mystery novel.

Papyri

This is the plural form of the Greek word *papyrus* (note "paper"). It was a form of writing material made from the papyrus plant which grew along the Nile river. A few such plants still may be seen there. While other forms of writing material were used—pottery, leather, metal—papyrus writings abound. The dry climate of Egypt and parts of Palestine were such as to preserve an amazing supply of papyri.

These writings were the language of everyday life—letters, commercial and legal documents, and the like. They throw a flood of light upon life of the times preceding, during, and after the life of Jesus.

Greek scholars had long recognized the difference between Classical Greek and that of the New Testament. So New Testament scholars referred to New Testament Greek. One German scholar, R. Rothe, called it "the language of the Holy Ghost [Spirit]." It was thought to be a special language given by the Holy Spirit for the recording of the New Testament.

But one day Adolf Deissmann of Berlin discovered that the language of the papyri was also the language of the New Testament. It was not a special language but the language used in everyday life by the common (*Koine*) people. Since then we speak of the New Testament language as *Koine* Greek.

This discovery has greatly enhanced our understanding of the New Testament. Somewhere I read that less than fifty words found in the New Testament have not been found in the papyri. In all likelihood these are words coined by Paul and other New Testament authors. This is especially typical of Paul. When he could not find a word to express an idea, he combined Greek words for the purpose.

Words are but pictures of ideas, sometimes of many ideas. Through the year I have found much rich preaching material by relating New Testament words to their multiple meanings in the papyri.

Dead Sea Scrolls

Insofar as biblical archaeology is concerned, one of its most priceless treasures was found purely by accident. It is called the "Dead Sea Scrolls." "In 1945 a Bedouin of the Ta-amireh tribe by the name of Muhammed al-Di'b was seeking a lost goat in the region [just west of the Dead Sea]. Noticing a cave he threw stones into it and heard something breaking. Going down into the cave he found pottery jars which he broke open. In one of these was some rolled leather with writing on it. This material he took to his home and kept for two years, then took to a dealer in antiquities at Bethlehem. These were the now-famous scrolls from Qumran Cave I."[5]

Altogether archaeologists have found six such caves. Some had less materials, but all in all they produced a "pearl" without price.

How did these things happen to be there? Not far from these caves and overlooking the Dead Sea was a colony of ascetic Jews called Essenes. In A.D. 70 near the end of the Jewish War they stored these literary treasures in these caves to protect them from the Roman soldiers. The manuscripts were sealed in large jars. That, plus the climate, preserved them for almost nineteen hundred years.

In the first cave "is a virtually complete copy of the book of Isaiah . . . [also] The Habakkuk Commentary [which] contains the first two chapters of the book of Habakkuk with a commentary accompanying the text."[6]

Finegan notes of Cave 4, "No less than tens of thousands of manuscript fragments were found here . . . Every book of the Hebrew Old Testament is represented except Esther . . . There are also thirteen manuscripts of Deuteronomy, twelve of Isaiah, ten of Pslams, seven of part of all of the Book of the Twelve Prophets, and five of books of the Pentateuch."[7]

Insofar as the New Testament is concerned, the writings of the Essenes themselves are important. For years a school of Christian scholars held that the thought patterns of the Gospel of John reflect Greek thinking in the second century A.D. But the thought patterns of John are also those found in the writings of the Essenes prior to A.D. 70 when these documents were placed in these caves. Thus the background of John's Gospel is Jewish, not Grecian, and supports the Johannine authorship of that Gospel.

Inscriptions
This term is used for writing found on monuments and other public structures. Some of these have shed light on problem passages, attesting to the accuracy of the Scriptures. One example will suffice.

In Acts 17:6 "rulers" renders the Greek work *politarchas,* "politarchs." Adverse critics denied that any Roman record showed that title was ever used for rulers in Thessalonica. But an inscription to the contrary has been found. The Via Egnatia (Egnatian Way) was a Roman international highway. It still forms the main street through modern Salonika (ancient Thessalonica).

The western entrance of this highway into Thessalonica was spanned by a Roman arch called the Vardar Gate. It stood until 1876. On it was an inscription, now in the British Museum, which begins with the words "In the time of the Politarchs . . ."

"It is probably to be dated somewhere between 30 B.C. and A.D. 143, while several other Thessalonian inscriptions, including one definitely dated in the reign of Augustus [B.C. 27-A.D.14], also mention Politarchs. This is of importance since in the Greek of Acts 17:6 the rulers of Thessalonica are called Politarchs. The term is otherwise unknown in extant Greek literature, but Luke's accuracy in the matter is entirely vindicated by the inscriptions."[8]

Thus far in this chapter brief references have been made to claims of adverse critics which were proved false by archaeology. In the remainder of the chapter we will look with more detail at three specific incidents of like kind.

Luke-Acts

Both of these books came from the pen of Luke. And no other New Testament writings have received more adverse criticism as to historical accuracy than Luke's writings. A. T. Robertson quotes the German scholar Baur's "extreme view" (Baur, *Paul*, Vol. I, p. 108) when he wrote that Luke's statements in Acts "can only be looked upon as intentional deviations from historic truth in the interest of the special tendency which they possess."[9]

It is ironic, however, that a former disciple of Baur, Sir William M. Ramsay, through archaeological research in Palestine and Asia Minor proved Baur and his school of thought to be completely wrong. The listing of some of his book titles attests this fact: *St. Paul the Traveller and Roman Citizen; The cities of St. Paul; Luke the Physician; Was Christ Born in Bethlehem?; The Bearing of Recent Discovery on the Trustworthiness of the New Testament.* As the result of his research Ramsay declared Luke to be one of the greatest of historians.

Before examining the one example chosen from Luke's writings, it is well to note that he was a physician-scientist-historian. As such, he knew how to do research, evaluate evidence, and draw sound conclusions. All this is reflected in Luke 1:1-4. And the verb tenses in this passage show that he did not at the outset tell what he proposed to do. He tells what he had done. Most likely he wrote his Gospel and then preceded the work with Luke 1:1-4.

Census Enrollment

Only Luke 2:1-7 tells how Jesus came to be born in Bethlehem (cf. Micah 5:2). It was due to an order by Caesar Augustus that his entire Empire be enrolled for the purpose of taxation. True to his historical sense, Luke notes that it was while Cyrenius (Quirinius) was governor of Syria. Everyone was to be enrolled in "his own city" (2:3) or native city. Joseph and Mary were of the lineage of David. So they had to travel from Nazareth to Bethlehem. Herod the Great died in 4 B.C. So Jesus' birth was prior to that date, probably 5 or 6 B.C. You may wonder how Jesus could have been born in 5 or 6 B.C. Here is how it happened. Christians have always believed that Jesus' birth divided history; but when the time of His birth was originally calculated, the calculator missed it by a few years.

Two problems confront us about Luke's reference to the enrollment. When was Quirinius governor of Syria? And was there an enrollment for taxation at all? These problems, like others raised about biblical accuracy, are rooted in a disposition not to accept the supernatural elements in the Scripture. In the case at hand it involves the biblical records of Jesus' virgin birth. Robertson says, "This prejudice [against the supernatural] led Baur and the [German] Tubingen school to deny that Luke wrote the Gospel and the Acts and to claim that the books were later party pamphlets of the second century."[10] It was with such unfounded prejudice that archaeologists had to contend.

The governorship of Quirinius is the most difficult problem in Luke 2:1-7. It hinges upon various references to his connections with Syria. Finegan points out three known dates in Quirinius' life: consulship in 12 B.C.; military expedition into Armenia in A.D. 3, when his base probably was Syria; his death in A.D. 21.[11]

Roman records show others as governors in Syria during the time covered by the first two dates. However, inscriptions have been found showing that it was possible to have two officials over given provinces at the same time. Finegan refers to such an inscription found at Tibur (Tivoli).[12] He also mentions a similar statement by the Jewish historian Josephus. It is possible that the one had charge of diplomatic matters, and the other was over military matters. Josephus speaks of "Saturninus and Volumnius, the presidents of Syria." Finegan adds, "Perhaps Quirinius was associated with Saturninus for a time in a similar way. If that were the case we would understand why Tertullian [an early Church Father] said that the census at the time of the birth of Jesus was 'taken in Judea by Sentius Saturninus.'"[13]

In fact Ramsay, on the basis of inscriptions, held that Quirinius was twice governor of Syria.[14] One of these inscriptions belongs to the date B.C. 10-7. This is most likely the governorship related to Jesus' birth. Augustus' decree could have been given in B.C. 8-7 and finally carried out in Judea in B.C. 6-5. Due to the Jews' hatred for paying taxes to a foreign power, Herod the Great could have delayed it as long as possible. Thus the weight of archaeological evidence favors Luke's account. His record for historical evidence should resolve any lingering questions at this point.

Furthermore, the adverse school of thought even questioned the making of such an enrollment. The idea of a household census was questioned, especially one which would require

Joseph and Mary to travel from their home in Nazareth to Bethlehem. But granting that such a census was taken, it is understandable that Herod, to placate the Jews, could have received permission to execute it on a tribal basis. But as early as 1930 Robertson wrote, "We have evidence for its [census] operation in both West and East, though most for the East."[15] And he quotes Ramsay to the effect that records in Egypt clearly show a household census. Ramsay notes one record which "gave a complete enumeration of all individuals who lived in the house, children, relatives, etc. In one case twenty-seven persons are enumerated in one paper by a householder."[16]

Evidence now points to the fact that beginning in B.C. 8-7 Rome inaugurated an enrollment system for purposes of taxation. They were taken every fourteen years. In Acts 5:37 Luke mentions the second such enrollment (A.D. 6) where he uses the Greek work for "taxing" (*apographe*) found in Luke 2:2.

In the Egyptian papyri actual records have been found for such an enrollment for taxation in Egypt, and in all likelihood throughout the Empire. They started in A.D. 34, then A.D. 48, another in A.D. 62—note the fourteen-year intervals. From then on, with some gaps, they run all the way to A.D. 202.

Virgin Birth and Resurrection

These do not fall into the realm of archaeology. But where archaeology has shed light upon disputed historical accuracy in Luke's writings, it has always proved him to be correct. He stands unchallenged as a reliable historian. It is fitting, therefore, that a brief word be said about these events which are alpha and omega, the beginning and the end, of God's redemptive work in the historical Christ.

As Paul's traveling companion, Luke most likely did his research for his Gospel (Luke 1:1-4) during Paul's two-year imprisonment in Caesarea. During this time he collected oral and written stories of events. He talked with eyewitnesses. It is even possible that he talked with Mary herself! To a physician more than to anyone else she would talk more freely about the conception and birth of Jesus.

All of Luke's Gentile training would tend to prejudice him against a virgin birth and a bodily resurrection from the dead. Yet, so convinced was he, that he wrote the most beautiful and complete accounts of both. His credibility as a historian has been tested and proved. And this fact undergrids the reliability of all other New Testament writings. Similar proofs are available in the Old Testament also.

Belshazzar

Daniel 5 relates the fall of Babylon to the Medo-Persians. Belshazzar is listed as "the king." He gave a massive banquet made famous by the handwriting on the wall (vv. 25-28). "In that night Belshazzar the king of the Chaldeans was slain" (v. 30).

This event became the prime target of adverse Old Testament critics in denying the historical value of the book of Daniel. All available records listed Nabonaid (Nabonidus) as the last king of

Babylon (555-539). Even the famous Cyrus Cylinder reads that his god Marduk "delivered into his hands Nabunaid, the king who did not worship him."[17] Also these critics said that, other than the book of Daniel, in all literature the name "Belshazzar" did not appear. They concluded that the name was purely fictional, invented by the author of Daniel.

However, we now know that Nabonaid shared the kingship with his eldest son Belshazzar. When the so-called Verse Account of Nabonaid was discovered, it tells the following story.

Nabonaid left Babylon and went westward to Tema which he conquered, killing its prince in battle. There he built a palace as beautiful as the one in Babylon. Also he made the town beautiful and built a wall about it.

Actually Belshazzar and his father shared a co-regency, the son in Babylon and the father in Tema. Thus Daniel 5 is correct when it says that Belshazzar was the last king of Babylon. Again, archaeology proved the critics wrong and the Bible correct.

Pool of Bethesda
John 5:1-9 records the healing of the lame man at the Pool of Bethesda (House of Mercy). The author says that it was near the place of the sheep. From Nehemiah we know where the Sheep Gate was located. Also the pool has "five porches" or colonnaded areas.

But again the adverse critics denied the location of such a pool. Some suggested that the site was at the Pool of Siloam or the Virgin's Fountain. They dated John's Gospel in the second

century, saying that it was written by an Elder
John of Ephesus who had only a tourist's knowledge of Palestine and Jerusalem. Their design
was to discredit the historical value of the Fourth
Gospel, insisting that it was only a theological
treatise.

But, again, archaeology entered the picture.
The Crusaders built shrines at holy places. In
the late 1880's a German archaeologist discovered the ruins of a Crusader shrine near the
spot where John located the pool of Bethesda.
Why the area was not excavated then is a mystery.

But in recent years such an excavation was
begun. In 1955, my wife and I visited the spot.
On subsequent trips to Jerusalem we followed
the progress of the excavation. The last time we
were there the work was nearing completion.
They had even posted a color drawing depicting
how it must have looked. It has the bases for five
porches, one on each of the four sides and one
down the middle forming two separate pools.
Beyond any question of doubt, this is the Pool of
Bethesda, exactly where the Fourth Gospel lo-
cates it!

Finegan describes the area thus. "The area
occupied was over five thousand square yards in
extent, the numerous fragments of columns and
capitals show that fine balustrades and galleries
surrounded the pools. Since these are in Roman
style, and since a Hebrew graffito found there
proves that the buildings were older than the time
of Hadrian, it may be supposed that the im-
pressive establishment was due to Herod the Great
and was constructed in connection with his work

on the Temple."[18] It was an imposing structure indeed!

But of even greater importance, it proves the historical value of the Fourth Gospel. Furthermore, it proves that its author was not a second-century tourist. He was someone familiar with the topography of Jerusalem prior to its destruction by the Roman Titus in A.D. 70. It points to a Palestinian author. It points to the Apostle John!

Truly, when adverse critics ceased to praise the Lord, the very "stones" continue to shout praise to Him.

4

The Bible:

The Old
Covenant

(Part 1)

Chapter 4
The Bible: The Old Covenant
Part 1

Chapters 4—7 of this book give a synopsis of the message of the Bible. The various volumes of a commentary will treat the books in detail. The purpose of these chapters is to take a broad view of these books of the Bible in order to see its overall message and purpose. This purpose is the working out in history of God's eternal redemptive purpose in Christ.

We speak of the Old and New Testaments. The word "testament" means "covenant." It is just as

---

In this chapter, you are reading about the following Old Testament books:

Genesis

Exodus

Leviticus

Numbers

Deuteronomy

To read about the other books in the Old Testament, read chapter 5.

correct to refer to the Old and New Covenants. While there are secondary covenants mentioned in the Bible, it centers largely in three major covenants: with Abraham (Gen. 12:1-3); with Israel (Ex. 19:1-8); and the new covenant in Christ (Jer. 31:31-34; Heb. 8).

This chapter deals with the first five books of the Bible. This body is commonly called the Pentateuch, from the Greek word for *five*. Some Old Testament scholars include Joshua in what they call the Hexateuch, from the Greek word for *six*. But Pentateuch seems to be a better division.

The Pentateuch traditionally is attributed to Moses as its author. There is a school of thought which sees these books as being written much later and by different authors. They date some of these books in the eighth century B.C. and/or also after the Babylonian exile. Both positions see these books as inspired by the Holy Spirit. I personally hold to the Mosaic authorship. But the purpose of this volume does not call for argument either way.

Genesis

"Genesis" is a Greek word for "beginning," or "origin." So Genesis is the book of "beginning" or "the origin of all things." The entire book is a credible historical document. Genesis 1—11 records true history. But it deals with vast eras of time which do not fit the dating system of historiography. Beginning with Abraham the remainder of the book is capable of historical dating.

Genesis 1—2 gives accounts of creation. The former is general; the latter is particular. I do not see these as coming from two different authors, but that the author moves from the general to the particular.

For instance, in Genesis 1 he uses the word *Elohim* for "God." This was the general name for God or gods. But in Genesis 2:4 he says, "The Lord God made the earth and the heavens (cf. Gen. 1:1). "Lord" translates *Yahweh* the name for the true God of Israel. The reading is *Yahweh Elohim*. The *Elohim* (God) who created was *Yahweh*.

Also Genesis 1:27 speaks of "male and female created he them." But Genesis 2:20-25 gives the details as to how they were of different sexes.

Pagan people had their complicated accounts of creation which involved their gods. The events in the Genesis account show that the one true God created all things. Only as people left the true God to worship false gods, they adapted the creation account to fit into their religious systems (cf. Rom. 1:21-32).

Some interpreters hold that man began by worshiping many gods and gradually evolved to the worship of one God. This is contrary to Genesis 1—2 and Romans 1. But in the early 1930's increasing evidence in both archaeology and anthropology showed that man began by worshiping one God and gradually began to worship many gods. This confirms the biblical record.

The Bible opens with "In the beginning God created the heavens and the earth" (Gen. 1:1). It does not date creation according to man's calendar. Should the various sciences *prove* that the

universe is billions of years old, it would not
change one bit the biblical record. It was "In the
beginning"—whenever that was (cf. John 1:1).

Some theologians and some scientists see conflict between Science and Genesis 1. However, if
you lay the basic conclusions of true Science
alongside the phases of creation in Genesis 1, it
is found that they agree. For example, both agree
that life began in water (Gen. 1:20-21). Note also
"after his [or "their"] kind" (Gen. 1:11-25), a reference to different species. The "days" of creation
present a problem for some. The Hebrew word
yom may refer to 24 hours, dawn to dusk, an
era, or an indefinite period of time, much as we
use "day." *Yom* is used three different ways in
Genesis 1.

Both the Bible and science agree that man is
the crown of creation. Unlike other creatures,
man is made in God's "image," not physical but
spiritual likeness (Gen. 1:26-27). The infinite
Person created man as a finite person capable of
direct dealings with God. And whether found in
a text or a test tube, all truth is of God.

In no sense does the Bible support the theory,
note that I said *theory*, of evolution. It is purely
an unproven theory. To present it as a fact is
within itself unscientific. The Bible teaches that
God created different species at different levels of
life. There is evidence of development within
given species. But there is no evidence, biblical
or otherwise, that one species ever ascended to a
higher level.

Science has done wonderful things. But by its
very nature it is incapable of dealing with ori-

gins. It deals with cause and effect. But science eventually comes to an effect for which there is no natural cause. It is at that point that we must take the leap of faith, something natural science cannot do. For faith falls in the realm of religion.

Many years ago I preached a sermon along this line. Noting the changeable nature of science, I said that any science textbook ten years old is obsolete. After the service a science teacher said to me, "Any textbook in science that is published is obsolete. We provide students with a textbook. But in order to keep abreast with the latest in scientific development, we teach from mimeographed materials provided daily."

The natural question arises. Are we going to rest our faith upon such, or upon the centuries-tested teachings of the Bible? The answer is obvious.

However, it should be noted that some of our greatest scientists are people who have strong religious faith. The late Arthur Compton, noted American physicist, not long before his death was quoted in a Chicago newspaper as saying that "In the beginning God" are the sublimest words ever penned.

George Washington Carver, noted black scientist of Tuskegee Institute, produced more products from the peanut than any other person. When asked by a reporter how he did it, he said, "I learned about it through an old book, the Bible." The reporter asked if the Bible told him about the peanut. He said, "No. The Bible told me about God, and God told me about the peanut."

Many years ago a young man came to my office. He was a graduate student in physics at Northwestern University. He said that the head of the physics department led him to Christ. Then he told the following story about this department head. He told his student that he came to Northwestern as a student who thought he knew all the answers to the matter of cause and effect. Thus he could trace all things back to origins. Then he said, "One day I was studying a specimen under a microscope. On its lens was a speck of dust. But I could not explain scientifically its cause. And that speck of dust led me to God."

Running through Genesis 1 is a theological theme. The Israelites had come out of Egypt where everything was a god: the Nile, insects and snakes, the sacred bull, the heavenly bodies, and Pharaoh. So, in effect, in his account of creation Moses is saying, "Do not worship these *things.* Worship the God who created them."

Genesis 3—4 tells of the temptation and fall of Adam and Eve and the consequences of doing Satan's will rather than God's will. Not only was their fellowship with God broken, but they were driven from the garden of Eden. Furthermore, Cain murdered his brother Abel. It is of interest to note God's first recorded question to man. "Where art thou?" (Gen. 3:9)—not geographically but spiritually. Also man's first question to God. "Am I my brother's keeper?" (Gen. 4:9).

It is significant to note in Genesis 4:25-26 the births of Seth and Enos, respectively the third son and grandson of Adam and Eve. Following the birth of Enos, "then began men to call upon

the name of the Lord" or *Yahweh*. The significance seems to be the establishment of a
spiritual line in contrast to the descendants of
Cain.

Genesis 6—9 relates the account of the flood.
Mankind, following the tendency toward sin, had
become so corrupt that they perished in the
flood—that is, all but righteous Noah and his
family. They were saved through the flood by
being in the ark which God had provided. Such
incidents in the Old Testament are called "types
of Christ"—provisions of salvation provided by
God that point to His greatest act of salvation in
Jesus Christ. Thus the Lord made a new beginning in His redemptive purpose.

As with creation, so it is that ancient pagans
also had their accounts of the flood which involved their gods. However, the same conclusion
holds true here. According to the rules of textual
studies, the Genesis account may be seen as the
original source.

But Genesis 11:1-9 shows that men, independent of God, sought to build a tower which
reached into heaven. Ironically, when they had
built as high as they could, God "came *down* to
see the city and the tower" (Gen. 11:5, author's
italics). To thwart man's ill-gotten purpose the
Lord sent a confusion of tongues. Instead of "one
language" (11:1), there were many. The result
was the scattering of people throughout the
earth.

Beginning with Genesis 11:27 the biblical
account comes into the realm of history which
submits to man's dating process. For Abram

(Abraham) may be dated about 2000-1900 B.C. He lived in Ur of the Chaldees, a city dedicated to moon worship. It is possible that Terah, Abraham's father, was a moon-worshipper. But there is no evidence that Abraham was such. Else how and why would he have answered the call of Jehovah?

Genesis 12:1-3 marks the beginning of God's working out His eternal redemptive purpose in the arena of history. To do so, He chose one man, Abraham. In doing so, He entered into the first of three covenants mentioned previously. It was a covenant of grace which called Abraham to a venture of faith. Considering the meaning of homeland and family to the ancients, it required an obedient faith beyond our comprehension. He left both, never to return. He did not know his destination, only that it was "a land that I would show thee." But the covenant contained a dual promise to bless Abraham and to make him a blessing. At the time, Abraham was 75 years old (v. 4) and had no children.

When he arrived in Canaan, God told Abraham that this was the land. So he claimed it for God (Gen. 12:7-8). For the first time the Lord spoke of giving this land to his "seed" (v. 7). This promise again called upon Abraham's faith since his wife Sarah was barren (Gen. 11:30), and both were beyond the age of child-bearing, (Gen. 15:1-6; Rom. 4). Paul points out that "seed" is singular and relates it to Christ (Gal. 3:16).

In the ancient world Canaan was a land-bridge joining the three known continents of that time—Europe, Africa, and Asia. It was to be the

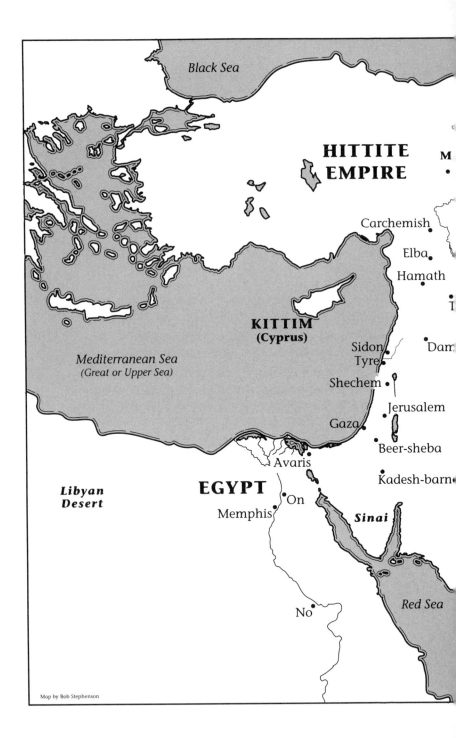

Black Sea

**HITTITE
EMPIRE**

M

Carchemish

Elba

Hamath

KITTIM
(Cyprus)

Sidon
Tyre

Dam

Shechem

Mediterranean Sea
(Great or Upper Sea)

Jerusalem

Gaza

Beer-sheba

*Libyan
Desert*

Avaris

Kadesh-barn

EGYPT

On

Memphis

Sinai

Red Sea

No

Map by Bob Stephenson

URARTU

Caspian Sea

NNI
n

• Nineveh

ASSYRIA

Tigris River

MEDIA

rates River

Mari •

or

BABYLONIA

• Susa

• Babylon

ELAM

DAR

Ur

Persian Gulf (Lower Sea)

ARABIA

• Dumah

• Tema

The Ancient World

• Dedan

| 0 | 100 | 200 | 300 | 400 |

Scale of Miles

base from which God's covenant people would reach the pagan world for Him. The same was true in New Testament times.

Eventually Isaac was born. And then Jacob. Jacob's twelve sons and their families became the twelve tribes of Israel. Joseph was Jacob's favorite son. Eventually through jealousy his brothers sold him into slavery in Egypt. And through a series of events he became second only to Pharaoh in power.

The events of Joseph in Egypt coincide with a period of the Hyksos reign in Egypt. "Hyksos" means "rulers of foreign lands." They were said to be of West Semitic stock, Syria-Palestine. They first introduced horse chariot warfare in Egypt. Using his powerful military force they drove the native Egyptian rulers southward. This Hyksos regime ruled in Egypt beginning in 1780 B.C. They were expelled from Egypt in about 1570-1545 (cf. Ex. 1:8).

The Hyksos people were Semites and thus related to the Israelites. This helps to explain Joseph's rise to power and also the welcome given to Jacob and his people when, at Joseph's request, they moved from Canaan to Egypt. They were settled in the land of Goshen, a choice area in northern Egypt. Jacob died in Egypt.

Joseph also died there. But his remembrance that Canaan was to be the covenant land of the Israelites is seen in his request that when they left Egypt his bones should be taken and buried in Canaan. This was done as he requested (Ex. 13:19). They were later buried by Joshua in Shechem, the portion of Canaan allotted to the children of Joseph (Josh. 24:32).

Exodus

Like "Genesis," the second book in the Old Testament was written in Hebrew, but its title comes from the Greek language. "Exodus" means a going out, exit, or departure. Obviously it refers to Israel's redemption from Egyptian bondage.

Exodus has a place in the Old Testament similar to that of the Gospels in the New Testament. All give emphasis to the compassion and redemptive work of God. God's revelation is tied firmly to history—with Moses in Exodus and Jesus in the Gospels. Not the picture of a covenant with those who follow the redeemer and proclaim the complete lordship of God (Christ).

With the political change in Egypt came a change in the life of the Israelites. During their stay in Egypt they had multiplied rapidly. So the new Pharaoh instituted a rash policy to curb their birthrate. He feared that in case of an invasion (by the Hyksos?) their enemy would find a ready ally in the Israelites (Ex. 1:8-10). When other measures failed, the order was given to kill all male babies at birth.

It was under this circumstance that Moses was born. But through a series of events, no doubt ordained by God, he was not killed. Instead, he wound up as the foster-child of Pharaoh's daughter, living in the palace of the ruler who would have destroyed him.

Moses' life may be divided into three forty-year periods: as a prince in Egypt, as a shepherd in Midian, and the period of the exodus. In Egypt he "was learned in all the widsom of the Egyptians, and was mighty in words and in deeds"

(Acts 7:22). In Midian he learned patience and the ways of the very land through which later he would lead the Israelites. Thus prepared, he had his "burning-bush" experience which sent him back to Egypt for the mission for which God had been preparing him.

The Egyptians regarded Pharaoh as a god. So the series of plagues was really a struggle between the one true God and the false god Pharaoh. The final plague, the death of all the first-born of the Egyptians, caused Pharaoh to permit the Israelites to leave Egypt. The miracle at the Red Sea defeated Pharaoh's abortive effort to veto his permission for the exodus. Thus Israel was delivered from both the land and the power of its ruler.

Three moons (months) after the exodus Israel arrived at Mt. Sinai (Ex. 19:1). It was there that God proposed to enter into the second key covenant with His redeemed people. In this case, however, it was a conditional covenant based upon obedience to the law. Note "if" and "then" (Ex. 19:5).

God, the greater party, laid down conditions which were to be met by the lesser party Israel. Until then God was not bound by His promise. Israel was to be a "peculiar [God's own] treasure." She was to be a priest-nation which would endeavor to bring pagan people to worship the true God.

Though Israel agreed to the terms (Ex. 19:8), subsequent history shows that she never fulfilled the *conditions.* So God was not bound by the *promise.* We will see that this refusal ultimately led to Israel's ruin and rejection as a covenant-people. But note that this covenant, unlike that with Abraham (Gen. 12), was sealed in animals' blood (Ex. 24).

Since this was a covenant of law, not of grace, Exodus 20:1-17 records the giving of the Ten Commandments, ten laws that were eternally true even before they were written in the Bible.

For the most part the remainder of Exodus is the record of the civil and religious legal systems revealed to Moses by God, the system of worship, and the dimensions and building of the tabernacle. But note the golden calf incident in Exodus 32.

Leviticus

"Leviticus" came to be the title of the third book of the Old Testament. It comes from the Greek translation of the Old Testament (Septuagint) which gave it the title *Levitikon*, "the Levitcal (book)."

Both Moses and Aaron were of the tribe of Levi (Ex. 2:1-2). Eventually this became the priestly tribe with Aaron as the first high priest (Ex. 28). And Leviticus is the book dealing with Levitical law governing worship, rites, and sacrifices.

Ronald Clements describes the book thus. "There is a close interweaving of instructions addressed to every Israelite with those which more particularly related to the priestly community."[1] Many of the regulations pertain to life among the Israelites which were to be taught and monitored by the priests as they were practiced in the daily life and health (Lev. 11) of the covenant community. In a very real sense this book is a call for Israel to be a holy people, one dedicated to God's

service. They are to be holy as He is holy, involv-
ing the ethical qualities of God (Lev. 11:44-45) as
well as being committed to His purpose.

Numbers

According to John Joseph Owens, "The title,
'Numbers,' is a translation of the title of the
Latin Vulgate, *Numeri*, or the Greek Septuagint,
Arithmoi [note 'arithmetic'] . . . 'Numbers' is
translated to refer to the two numberings which
are recorded in chapters 1—4 and 26."[2] The remainder of the book is related to other events in
Israel's life, especially her wanderings in the wilderness.

Owens outlines the book thus.

1. At Sinai. Preparations are made for the
journey of unknown duration (1:1—10:10).

2. From Sinai to the Wilderness of Paran
(10:11—20:29).

3. The approach east of the Dead Sea (21:1—
36:13).[3]

The most important event in the book is found
in chapters 13—14. From Mt. Sinai Moses led
Israel to Kadesh-barnea, the southern entrance
into Canaan. The Lord was ready to lead His
people into the "Promised Land." So Moses sent
spies, one from each tribe, to spy out the land
(Num. 13). Upon their return they gave a glowing
report. It was a land flowing with milk and
honey, a symbol of fertility and prosperity (v. 27).
But 10 of the spies also pointed out its walled
cities and giant people. The implication was that
they could not conquer it. This greatly chilled
the enthusiasm of the people. But Caleb (v. 30),
later joined by Joshua (14:6-9), urged that they

could take it. "If the Lord delight in us, then he will bring us into this land . . . Only rebel not ye against the Lord, neither fear ye the people of the land, for they are bread for us [we would say 'a piece of cake']: their defence is departed from them, and the Lord is with us: fear them not" (14:8-9).

The people accepted the majority report. They murmured against Moses and Aaron, even threatened to stone them, Caleb, and Joshua to death. They said that it would have been better to die in Egypt or in the desert. Actually they wanted to select a new leader and return to Egypt. Totally forgotten was the covenant at Mt. Sinai.

As punishment for this rebellion God said that everyone of them 20 years and older, except Caleb and Joshua, would not enter Canaan. Instead, they would wander in the desert until all that group died. Then He would take a new generation into the land.

For this "the people mourned greatly" (14:39). Apparently they decided that it would be better to die in the conquest of Canaan than to wander in the desert the rest of their lives. But the next morning they told Moses they had changed their minds [repented] about Canaan. They were ready to invade the land. But, in effect, Moses said, "It is too late. God has decreed." Thus began the long years of aimless wandering.

In effect God said that He had redeemed them from Egyptian bondage. They belonged to Him. They could not undo that redemption. Theirs was not a case of lost redemption but of lost opportunity.

Deuteronomy

"Deuteronomy" is a Greek word meaning "a second law" or a "second giving of the law." By many it is said to be the book of the law found in the temple during the religious reforms under Josiah (2 Kings 22:8). From this some scholars hold that the book of Deuteronomy actually was written at this time (8th century B.C.). However, Jews from the fourth century B.C. regarded this book as the last book of the Pentateuch. I hold to this view.

More than 25 years ago I asked an Old Testament scholar his opinion as to who wrote Deuteronomy. He replied, "I think that except for certain editorial additions Moses was the author." Someone other than Moses wrote the last chapter, since it describes his death and burial. This chapter probably was written by Joshua.

The book is composed of sermons preached by Moses designed to prepare the Israelites for entering Canaan. The Canaanites had the most depraved of religions. It involved both the worship of sex deities and child sacrifice. Israel would be most tempted by the former. Even two kings were guilty of the latter. So God warns against both.

Furthermore, Deuteronomy involves a renewal of Israel's Covenant with God. John D. W. Watts says, "Chapters 5—30 especially proclaim this invitation to covenant or covenant renewal."[4] Note the Ten Commandments in 5:7-21.

Deuteronomy 6:4-5 summarizes the message of the book. "Hear, O Israel: The Lord [Yahweh] our God is one Lord: And thou shalt love the Lord thy God with all thine heart, and with all thy soul, and with all thy might."

Of interest is the fact that in His wilderness temptations Jesus quoted only from Deuteronomy. It is tragic that in her Canaan temptation Israel did not remember and live by this book.

5

The Bible:

The Old Covenant

(Part 2)

Chapter 5
The Bible: The Old Covenant
Part 2

When you turn the page from Deuteronomy to Joshua you enter a new era in Israel's history. The years of wandering are over. God said, "Moses my servant is dead" (Josh. 1:2). Henceforth the nation is to be led by Joshua, the Lord's choice to succeed Moses. She is now ready to enter Canaan, the land of her destiny.

Joshua-Ruth

This period covers the time from Israel's entrance into Canaan until shortly before the

---

In this chapter, you are reading about the following Old Testament books:

Joshua	Proverbs	Amos
Judges	Ecclesiastes	Obadiah
Ruth	Song of Solomon	Jonah
1 and 2 Samuel	Isaiah	Micah
1 and 2 Kings	Jeremiah	Nahum
1 and 2 Chronicles	Lamentations	Habakkuk
Ezra	Ezekiel	Zephaniah
Nehemiah	Daniel	Haggai
Esther	Hosea	Zechariah
Job	Joel	Malachi
Psalms		

To read about the other books in the Old Testament, read chapter 4.

twelve tribes of Israel became a united people under a king.

"Joshua" means "God (Yahweh) is salvation." It was he who led Israel out of the wilderness into the more stable life of Canaan. Of interest is the fact that "Jesus" is the Greek equivalent of Joshua. As Joshua led Israel out of the wilderness into the "Promised Land," so Jesus leads believers in Him out of the wilderness of lostness into the kingdom of God.

Space does not permit a thorough analysis of the remaining books of the Old Testament. Suffice it to say that the book of Joshua relates Israel's conquest of Canaan. After the conquest the tribes settled in their allotted territories. They came together only when threatened by some outside danger.

However, Israel did not completely conquer and destroy the Canaanites. Instead, they settled down among them. The result was what Moses feared most (cf. Deuteronomy). Instead of leading the Canaanites to worship God, the Israelites were paganized by them. This was especially true following the death of Joshua.

Judges may be outlined as follows: Israel sinned, God punished; Israel repented, God delivered; Israel sinned, etc. This book gets its name from the fact that when Israel was beset by their enemies, God raised up a "judge" to deliver her. Completely forgotten was Israel's covenant with God at Sinai.

Ruth probably had its setting during the latter part of the period of Judges. It is a story of normal life during this turbulent period. It reflects family tragedy, loyalty, and love. Ruth became the great grandmother of David (Ruth 4:21-22).

Of interest is the fact that because of their heroic deeds, Rahab, a Canaanite (Joshua 2:1), and Ruth, a Moabite, are mentioned in the genealogy of Jesus (Matt. 1:5-6). Both had become worshippers of the true god.

1 and 2 Samuel

Ben F. Philbeck, Jr., says that "the narratives in Samuel may legitimately be considered Israel's history of the establishment and development of a united monarchy over Israel and Judah."[1]

Samuel was born in answer to the prayers of his mother Hannah (1 Sam. 1). In keeping with her promise, from early childhood he served in the tabernacle. As a lad God called him to be a judge in Israel (1 Sam. 3). He has been called Israel's last judge and first prophet. Philbeck notes that he was a young man when Shiloh, the site of the tabernacle, was destroyed about 1050 B.C. Solomon became Israel's king between 971 and 961 B.C. So 1 Samuel covers a period of about 100 years.[2]

Chapter 8 marks a definite turn in Israel's history. The heads of the tribes requested that Samuel give them a king, "that we also may be like all the nations" (8:20). In Exodus 19 God said that they were to be a nation set apart. They were a theocracy, ruled by God who gave His rule through chosen servants. Now they wanted to be like their pagan neighbors.

When Samuel objected, God told him to give them a king. "They have not rejected thee, but

Ark of the Covenant

they have rejected me, that I should not reign over them" (8:7). Not only had they forgotten the covenant; they had rejected God Himself. So Samuel gave them a king.

Saul was the first king of Israel (1 Sam. 9-10), but he proved to be a great disappointment. So God told Samuel to go to Bethlehem to the house of Jesse where he was to anoint a new king (1 Sam. 16:1-13). The choice was David, so Samuel anointed him to become the new king. However, he did not actually assume this role until Saul's death. In the meantime Saul repeatedly tried to kill David.

After Saul's death David became king over Judah (2 Sam. 2:4). The other tribes formed another kingdom with Saul's son Ishbosheth as king. He reigned only two years (2 Sam. 2:8-10). Eventually all the tribes accepted David as king. He reigned for 40 years, 7½ years in Hebron and the remainder in Jerusalem (2 Sam. 5:4-5).

He became a successful king in Israel, extending its borders until it became the most powerful nation in the Middle East.

God promised that David would have an everlasting kingdom (2 Sam. 7:16). This promise was not fulfilled in Solomon or other of his earthly descendants, but in Jesus Christ who was born in David's line.

David was a man of God. But he succumbed to temptation in his sin with Bathsheba (2 Sam. 11-12). His guilt of adultery and murder was exposed by Nathan the prophet. As punishment, the rest of his life was filled with sorrow and trouble (2 Sam. 12:1-24). The remainder of 2

Samuel gives details of this, including the rebellion of David's son Absalom.

1 Kings-2 Chronicles

According to M. Pierce Matheney, Jr. originally 1 and 2 Kings were one book with the Hebrew title which means "Kings."[3] They were printed in the Hebrew Bible as one book until the 16th century A.D. In the Greek translation of the Old Testament (Septuagint) it is written on two scrolls. Thus it comes to us as 1 and 2 Kings. And they are just that in the account of the kings of Israel and Judah.

First and Second Kings cover the period of history from the reign of Solomon until the Babylonian captivity in 587 B.C. Following the death of Solomon the kingdom divided. The ten northern tribes followed Jeroboam I to form the northern kingdom of Israel. Judah and Benjamin remained loyal to Rehoboam, Solomon's son, to form the southern kingdom of Judah. Israel fell to the Assyrians in 722 B.C.

Following the division these books relate the intermingled history of both kingdoms.

First and Second Chronicles contain material found in the books of Samuel and Kings. But the Chronicles also emphasize the history of Judah and temple worship.

Ezra-Esther

Ezra relates the return of a remnant of Jews from the Babylonian exile and the building of a new temple. This was done under two difficulties: opposition of Jersualem's neighbors and the low spiritual condition of the Jews.

Nehemiah tells of the rebuilding of the walls of Jerusalem. He held the important position of cupbearer to the Persian king Artaxerxes. From him he received permission and aid for this enterprise. Nehemiah also effected religious and social reforms in Jerusalem.

Esther is the beautiful story of her part in effecting the deliverance of the Jews from extermination plotted by Haman. Its best known words are "who knoweth whether thou art come to the kingdom for such a time as this? (4:14)" The Jewish feast of Purim celebrates this deliverance.

Job-Song of Solomon

Many scholars regard the book of Job as one of the oldest pieces of literature in existence. It is presented as a drama (Prologue, Job 1—2; Dialogue, Job 3—41; Postlude, Job 42).

Job refutes the ancient idea that a given punishment (suffering) is due to a given sin, an idea which persists today with many people.

In this book we see a threefold expression of God's will: Intentional will (He wills to bless His people); Circumstantial will (God wills that we trust Him under adverse circumstances); Ultimate will (God's intention ultimately will be done as seen in God's blessings in the end).

Psalms were written to be sung by the Hebrews. Approximately 70 Psalms are attributed to David. The remainder had other authors. The Psalms run the gamut of man's emotions and experiences.

Procession of Worship to the Temple

Proverbs is a book of proverbs. A proverb is a brief statement of truth related to practical living. Solomon "spake three thousand proverbs" (1 Kings 4:32). This proverbial method of teaching originated in the East.

Ecclesiastes relates the search for the true meaning of life. This is not found in *things.* All such are "vanity" (fleeting, passing). The conclusion is "Fear (reverence) God, and keep his commandments: for this is the whole *duty* of man" (12:13). "Duty" (KJV) is in italics, showing that it is not in the Hebrew text. So "the whole of man."

Song of Solomon is ascribed to Solomon. It depicts the pure love between a man and a woman. But many believe it is intended to show God's love for His people.

Isaiah-Daniel

These are called the Major Prophets. This refers to their length rather than to their relative importance.

Isaiah was one of four great prophets of the eighth century B.C. Isaiah and Micah prophesied in Judah and Amos and Hosea prophesied in Israel. This was a turbulent period in which the two great empires, Assyria and Egypt, struggled for supremacy. Israel and Judah were caught in the middle. In addition to this, the people of the two nations were corrupted by paganism.

Isaiah himself was a highly educated man, possibly a member of royalty. He was the poet among the prophets.

For the most part Isaiah 1—39 sounds the

note of judgment. (Chapters 7, 9, and 11 prophesy concerning Christ and His kingdom.)
Isaiah 40—66 sounds the note of hope. Chapters
42—53 contain the wonderful Suffering Servant
passages concerning Christ. This prophet predicts the captivity of both Israel and Judah. He
also predicts the return of Judah from the
Babylonian exile.

"The book is one of the world's greatest master-
pieces. Composed by an educated man in the
purest Hebrew, it is elevated in style, vehement
in expression, fervent in feeling, and vivid in its
imagery. It is more widely quoted in the New
Testament than any other book."3

Jeremiah reflects a sad time in Judah. It
covers the closing years of the Southern Kingdom in the seventh and sixth centuries B.C.
Jeremiah is sometimes called the "weeping
prophet" as he wept over the nation's idolatry.
But he also sounds a message of hope for the
future following the Babylonian captivity.

Jerusalem and its temple were destroyed by
Nebuchadnezzar in 587 B.C. Most of the leading
people were taken into exile. Because Jeremiah
advised surrender to the Babylonians he was regarded as a traitor to his nation. In fact, he was
her most loyal patriot.

Lamentations is Jeremiah's lament over the
destroyed city of Jerusalem. It describes the
ruined city and the cause of its desolation. "The
book has been called a funeral dirge over
Jerusalem."4

Ezekiel in dramatic form describes the sins of
Judah and the destruction of Jerusalem. He was

among those taken into exile in 598 B.C. He
ministered to the exiles in Babylon and predicted
a glorious future for Judah. Chapter 37 depicts
the future hope for God's people in the figure of
the "dry bones."

Daniel's prophecy was made in Babylon. It is
one of the great apocalyptic books in the Bible.
"Apocalyptic" describes literature written in a
code language used by the Jews in time of trouble. Daniel 5 relates the fall of Babylon to the
Medo-Persians.

Its visions provide fascinating and meaningful
reading. For instance, the four beasts (Dan. 7:3)
are regarded by many as the four great world
empires—Babylonian, Medo-Persian, Greco-
Macedonian, and Roman. Daniel 8 depicts the
conquest of Alexander the Great. Chapter 9 is
seen as the Messianic kingdom of Christ. Chapters 10—12 refer to events connected with the
end of the age or time.

The Minor Prophets

As previously noted, these twelve prophecies
are *minor* only as to length. Each is a message
from God.

Hosea is a prophecy delivered to the northern
kingdom of Israel in the eight century B.C. Kyle
M. Yates, Sr. called it "a succession of sobs."

Chapters 1—3 tell of Hosea's heartbreaking experience over the infidelity of his wife Gomer. Yet
God told him to redeem her by purchasing her at
the slave market and to take her back as his
wife. From this the prophet was able to understand God's love for adulterous Israel. The
remainder of Hosea is a denunciation of the peo-

ple for their idolatry and other sins. Since God pictures Himself as Israel's husband, the message of Hosea is most appropriate.

Joel largely contains three messages: (1) the calamity caused by a plague of locusts; (2) God's answer to the prayers of the people; and (3) a prophecy that the Jews will eventually build a great nation in Palestine. Joel 2:28-32 may be seen as the text for Peter's sermon at Pentecost (Acts 2:16-21).

Amos records the prophecy of Amos of Judah to the northern kingdom of Israel in the eighth century B.C. The prophet condemns the idolatrous worship at Bethel and Dan, the oppression of the poor by the rich, and predicts the Assyrian exile which began in 722 B.C.

In Amos 9:8 he calls Israel "the sinful (unlawful) kingdom." The meaning seems to be that this kingdom, founded in rebellion, is not a part of God's redemptive purpose. That purpose runs through Judah and the lineage of David.

Obadiah is the prophecy of that prophet who lived in Jerusalem during the Babylonian exile. As God's messenger he prophesied the doom of Edom, descendants of Esau, who had rejoiced over Judah's fall to the Babylonians. He also prophesied that at some future time Jews would again rule over David's kingdom.

Jonah is one of the greatest missionary books of the Bible. Jonah was a citizen of the northern kingdom of Israel. God told him to go to Nineveh, Assyria's capital and prophesy that unless it repented it would be destroyed in 40 days. Since Assyria was Israel's enemy, Jonah thought that he would be a traitor to deliver such a warning.

Failing to escape, Jonah obeyed the Lord's command. Nineveh repented and was spared. Even so, the prophet pouted over the outcome. Jonah teaches God's love for all people.

Micah belongs to the "big four" prophecies in the eighth century B.C. Like Isaiah he prophesied in Judah, condeming her idolatry and the oppression of the poor by the rich. Just prior to the fall of Israel in 722 B.C., Micah prophesied the destruction of both Israel and Judah. He also prophesied that Jesus would be born in Bethlehem (5:2).

Nahum begins with the words "The burden of Nineveh." It is a prophecy concerning the destruction of Nineveh in 612 B.C. It presents both the Judge, God, and then His judgment upon the city. Other than this, very little is known about Nahum himself.

Habakkuk prophesied in Judah in the latter half of the seventh century B.C., probably also in the opening years of the sixth century. He was a contemporary of Jeremiah. He wonders why God delays judgment upon Judah for her sins. But he predicts her fall to the Chaldeans or Babylonians. Also he condemns the sins of Babylon and predicts her ultimate fall. Though he wonders about God's delay, he closes his book with a prayer of faith.

Zephaniah also was a contemporary of Jeremiah, Habakkuk, and Nahum. Like them, he denounced the sins of Judah, prophesied her judgment and that of neighbor nations. Also he predicted blessings upon Jerusalem following the Babylonian exile.

Haggi and *Zechariah* both prophesied in Jerusalem. Due to opposition encountered by Ezra and Zerubbabel, building of the temple had been delayed. So these two prophets sought to stir up the people to get on with the project.

In addition Zechariah 9—14 deals with God's everlasting kingdom; it is a picture of the kingdom of Christ. John D. W. Watts says of Zechariah, "The themes are: salvation, advent, and the kingdom of God."[5]

Malachi was the last of the Old Testament prophets. Judah was under Persian rule. Even though the temple had been built, the people had become lax in their religious duties. This was evident in the type of offerings the people made to God.

Though this book contains many more wonderful things, it is probably best known for its message on stewardship and tithing (3:7-12). However, its greatest message is related to the coming of the Messiah (Chapter 4). The last of the Old Testament prophets points to God's full revelation in His Son Jesus Christ. The next prophetic voice heard in the Bible will be John the Baptist heralding that the One toward whom the Old Covenant points has come—Jesus of Nazareth, son of Mary, Son of God.

The Bible:

The New Covenant

(Part 1)

Chapter 6
The Bible: The New Covenant
Part 1

We come now to the third of the major covenants of the Bible. When it became evident that Israel would not fulfill the conditional covenant made at Mt. Sinai, God promised a new covenant (Jer. 31:31-34). Hebrews 8 says that this promised covenant was fulfilled in Jesus Christ. Like the grace covenant made with Abraham (Gen. 12:1-3), so this new covenant is one of grace. It, therefore, is actually a fulfillment of the covenant made with Abraham. As previously noted, Paul

---

In this chapter, you are reading about the following New Testament books:

Matthew

Mark

Luke

John

Acts

To read about the other books in the New Testament, read chapter 7.

---

says that Abraham's "seed" (singular) is Christ (Gal. 3:16). In chapters 6—7 we will deal with the New Covenant or Testament.

The Interbiblical Period

As you turn the page from Malachi to Matthew, you span a period of about four hundred years. In Malachi the Jews were living under Persian rule. In Matthew they were under Roman rule.

The "Interbiblical Period" is the period between the Old and New Testaments. Alexander the Great conquered the Persian Empire in 331 B.C. At his death in 321 B.C. his empire was broken up into five kingdoms. The two which touch upon the biblical record were the Ptolomy kingdom in Egypt and the Seleucid kingdom whose capital city was Antioch in Syria. Antiochus Epiphanes (the Glorious) ruled over the Seleucid kingdom 175-164 B.C. One of his goals was to force Greek culture and religion on the Jews. While he had some success in Galilee, he had virtually none in Judea.

Finally, to show his contempt for the Jews, he sacrificed a sow on the sacred altar in the Jewish temple in Jerusalem. The sow was boiled in water. Then what A. T. Robertson called "sow juice" was sprinkled on the walls of the temple. Since hogs were unclean to the Jews, this totally defiled the temple. It was later cleansed and re-dedicated. The feast of Dedication commemorated this event (John 10:22).

This series of persecutions precipitated a revolt led by Judas Maccabeus in which the Jews won their independence in 163 B.C. Judea remained an independent nation until 63 B.C. At this time the Roman general Pompey with his army was in northern Palestine. He was invited to settle a dispute over who should be high priest in Jerusalem. This opened the door whereby Pompey took over Palestine for the Romans. Thus Palestine was under Roman rule at the time Jesus was born.

The Synoptic Gospels

"Synoptic" comes from a Greek word which means "seeing together." This word is used of Matthew, Mark, and Luke. In large measure they present the life of Jesus from the same point of view. Most interpreters see Mark as the first Gospel to be written. Matthew and Luke follow Mark's material, though not always in the same chronological order. Yet both Matthew and Luke contain material not found in Mark. At the same time Luke contains material not found in the other two Synoptic Gospels (9:51—18:14).

Each of these Gospel writers wrote with a particular group in mind. Luke, a Gentile, wrote to his friend or sponsor Theophilus, with the Gentile world in view. Thus he began by stating his method of research. Mark wrote to a Roman readership. They were more concerned with Jesus' actions than His teachings. So he plunged immediately into His ministry. With the word "straightway" or "immediately" he moved from one deed to another. Matthew wrote to a Jewish readership to prove that Jesus was the Messiah. To do so he began with Jesus' genealogy which was important to the Jews. He followed Joseph's genealogy, but was careful to show that Joseph was not Jesus' real father (1:16). Luke gave His genealogy from the standpoint of Mary (3:23-38). Repeatedly Matthew mentioned events in Jesus' life as fulfillment of Old Testament messianic prophesies.

Both Matthew and Luke relate Jesus' virgin birth; Matthew from the standpoint of Joseph (1:18-25), Luke from the standpoint of Mary (1:26-38). Both Matthew and Luke record Jesus' temptations in the wilderness (Matt. 4; Luke 4). Mark merely takes note of this without details. Both Matthew and Luke record the Sermon on the Mount (Matt. 5—7; Luke 6). But Matthew's account is longer and smoother to read.

One distinct characteristic of the Synoptic Gospels is that, following Jesus' baptism and temptations, they center His ministry in Galilee and environs. Luke 9:51—18:14 is peculiar to that Gospel. It records a Judean ministry which is not reported elsewhere. The only visit to Jerusalem in Jesus' ministry recorded in the Synoptics is His final one. Luke places a greater emphasis on Jesus' prayer life than any of the other Gospels.

All three Synoptic writers were inspired of the Holy Spirit. But each author was free to arrange the material according to his purpose. For instance, Matthew does not always follow the chronological order of the others. He arranges his material in blocks to show various aspects of Jesus as the King-Messiah.

The Fourth Gospel

The Fourth Gospel was written in Ephesus sometime during A.D. 80-90. The traditional author is the Apostle John, a tradition that has been affirmed by archaeology. John's stated purpose in writing is found in John 20:31. "But these are written, that ye might believe that Jesus is the Christ, the Son of God; and that believeing ye might have life through his name." Therefore, John stresses both the deity of Jesus and the humanity of Christ.

John wrote in opposition to a pagan philosophy known as Gnosticism from the Greek word for "knowledge." The Gnostics sought to explain the origin of the material universe. They held that God is absolutely good and matter absolutely evil. So how could such a God create such a universe? In an effort to answer this question the Gnostics imagined a series of beings coming out of God in descending order. Each had less deity than the one above it. The last one had enough deity to create, but so little as to be able to create evil matter.

When the Gnostics came into contact with Christianity they identified Christ as the lowest being in their system. Gnostics were divided into two groups. The Docetic Gnostics (from *dokeo*, "I seem") said that Christ had no flesh and blood body; He only seemed to have one. They denied the humanity of Christ. The Cerinthian Gnostics (named after their leader Cerinthus) held that Christ was not born, neither did He die. The divine Christ came upon Jesus at His baptism and left Him on the cross. They denied the deity of Jesus. The entire Gnostic system cut through the Christian faith. Anyone today who denies the humanity of Christ and/or the deity of Jesus is a neo-Gnostic! So John wrote to refute this heresy (see also Colossians; 1 John).

John's format for his Gospel is to build it about seven "signs" (miracles) of Jesus which declare His deity. And his secondary purpose in writing was to supplement the Synoptic accounts. He neither challenges nor changes their accounts, but he does supplement them by adding material not found in them. He only parallels them in the miracle of feeding the multitude (see John 6) and beginning with Jesus' final week before Calvary and continuing through the resurrection. He parallels the feeding of the five thousand to show the cause of the collapse of Jesus' Galilean ministry.

If we had only the Synoptic Gospels it would appear that the first time Jesus visited Jerusalem in His public ministry He was crucified. But John shows four previous visits before the final one. In each of these the antagonism of the Jewish leaders increased. Matthew and Mark do not report a Judean ministry. But Luke 9:51—18:14 and John 7—10 join in recording a ministry in Jerusalem and Judea which precedes Jesus' final week before the cross. We are truly in John's debt for providing material which gives a well-rounded Gospel record.

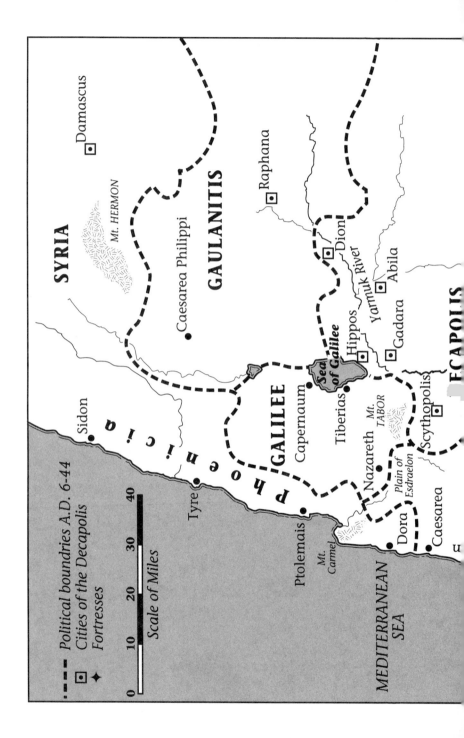

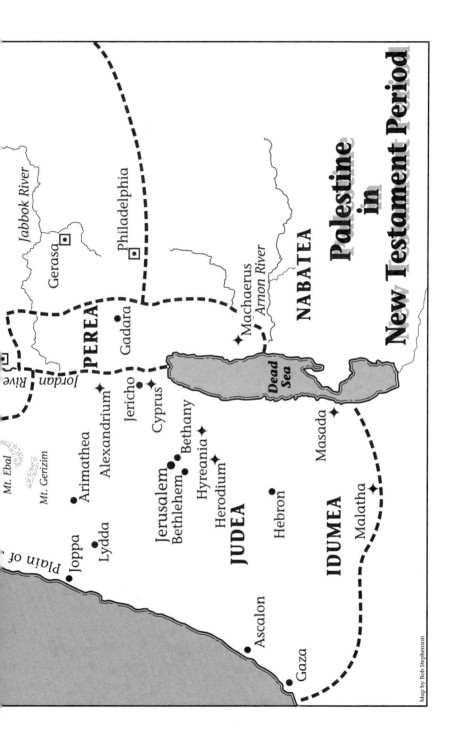

Palestine in New Testament Period

Map by Bob Stephenson

Acts

The book of Acts was also written by Luke. Like his Gospel it is addressed to Theophilus (see Luke 1:3). It is possible that he was a Christian friend or even Luke's sponsor in his research and writing of Luke-Acts.

Luke is the only Gentile writer in the New Testament. He was probably a citizen of Philippi in Macedonia. He may have been led to Christ by Paul in Troas. Many interpreters see Luke as the man of Macedonia in Paul's vision by which he received the "Macedonian Call" (Acts 16:9). Beginning in Acts 16:10 is the "we" section of Acts, showing that in Troas Luke became a travelling companion of Paul. Years later Paul referred to Luke as his "beloved physician" (Col. 4:14). And he stayed with Paul to the end (2 Tim. 4:11).

Paul was in prison in Caesarea for two years. It is altogether probable that it was during this time that Luke did his research for his Gospel and for Acts 1—12. Acts 13:1—16:8 could have come to Luke through Paul, including Paul's conversion experience and subsequent events in which Paul was a participant. Of course, the "we" section would be known to Luke from personal experience. Research does not negate divine inspiration. The Holy Spirit guided the writers in the research as well as the writing (Luke 1:1-4).

Acts probably was written in the latter half of Paul's Roman imprisonment. That Luke leaves Paul a prisoner probably indicates that he wrote Acts prior to A.D. 63. Though not certain, some think that Luke planned a third book.

Why did Luke write Acts? Some see it as an apologetic that he wrote to be used in Paul's defense before Caesar. Frank Stagg[1] makes a good case for Luke writing an account of the struggle for "an unhindered gospel." One thing is certain. He has given us a wonderful account of the spread of the gospel in the first century A.D.

That Luke intended to relate Acts to his Gospel is evident in Acts 1:1-5. The events marking the close of the gospel overlap into his second book. Luke-Acts places great emphasis upon the work of the Holy Spirit in Jesus and in His followers (1:8). "All that Jesus began both to do and teach" was carried forward as the Spirit worked through the Christian people.

In Jewish life Pentecost celebrated the beginning of the grain harvest. In Christian life it marks the general harvest of souls through the redemption provided by God in Christ. Jesus had promised to be with His people as they carried out the Great Commission (Matt. 28:18-20). He kept this promise through His Spirit (Rom. 8:9).

It was at Pentecost that the apostles first fully understood the meaning of Jesus' death and resurrection. Also, from like scared rabbits hiding in their holes, they became bold as lions. At Pentecost one Spirit-powered sermon by Peter led three thousand souls to Jesus (2:41). Then five thousand more *men* (4:4)! Luke does not say how many *women*. Peter and John defied the persecution and authority of the Sanhedrin (4:19-20).

Following Stephen's death (7:60), the first Christian martyr, a general persecution was led by Saul of Tarsus. But it only scattered the seed of the gospel as Christians went everywhere preaching the word (8:4). Following Saul's (Paul's) conversion experience this immediate persecution ceased.

In Acts 8, 10—11 we see evidence of the spread of the gospel: to half-Jews or Samaritans, to an Ethiopian eunuch, to Cornelius, a Roman, who was studying and practicing the Jewish religion and to pagan Gentiles in Antioch. The careful investigation of each case, except the eunuch, shows how reluctantly the Jerusalem church accepted these new developments. In fact, that church did little to help Gentile missions, other than to agree that Paul and Barnabas "should go to the heathen" (Gal. 2:9). For this reason the center of the Christian movement shifted to Antioch.

Acts 12 records the martyr's death of James the brother of John at the hand of Herod Agrippa I (vv. 1-2). He was the first apostle to die as a martyr. This chapter also records the death of Herod Agrippa I (vv. 20-23).

Acts 13—14 tell of a decidedly new development when the church in Antioch, at the Holy Spirit's command, sent Paul and Barnabas as missionaries to Cyprus and to Asia Minor (Perga, Pisidian Antioch, Iconium, Lystra, and Derbe) where they encountered considerable opposition.

Upon their return to Antioch in Syria they learned that Judaizers (Jewish Christians of the sect of the Pharisees, 15:1,5) had stirred up con-

siderable trouble in the church. They said that
Gentiles must first become Jewish proselytes,
then believe in Jesus to be saved. Paul and Barnabas had preached salvation by grace through
faith. The Judaizers preached a message of
works plus faith.

To decide this issue the first Christian conference met in Jerusalem (Acts 15; Gal. 2). The
decision supported Paul and Barnabas. But the
Judaizers continued to hound Paul's footsteps.
Having lost on doctrinal grounds they opposed
him on personal ones.

Back in Antioch, Paul and Barnabas had a
sharp difference over John Mark. He had turned
back on the first missionary journey. So Paul
opposed taking him again. Barnabas took Mark
and went to Cyprus. Paul chose Silas and went
on his second missionary journey (Acts
15:36-41).

At Lystra, Paul chose a young man, Timothy,
to join in the missionary work (16:1-3). Paul's
purpose was to go to Ephesus. But the Holy
Spirit guided him to Troas and thence to Philippi
in Europe. Of interest is the fact that every new
development in Acts in the spread of the gospel
was either at the command of the Holy Spirit or
with His approval. Already in Rome there was a
Christian church. This fact marked the beginning of Paul's campaign to take Europe for
Christ.

Beaten and imprisoned in Philippi, run out of
Thessalonica, accepted in Berea, and laughed
out of Athens, Paul finally arrived in Corinth
where he ministered for eighteen months (Acts

18:1). He came to Corinth "in weakness, and in fear, and in much trembling" (1 Cor. 2:3). And well he might do so.

Corinth was the commercial capital of the Roman empire. Its chief deity was the sex goddess Aphrodite whose temple stood on the Acrocorinthus (High Place of Corinth) eighteen hundred feet above sea level. Corinth was also a cesspool of evil. "To Corinthianize" was to sink to the lowest moral depths. Would the gospel work there?

Since coming to Europe, Paul had had trouble wherever he went. Probably he was wondering if he had made a mistake in leaving Asia. But in a night vision the Lord said, "Be not afraid, but speak, and hold not thy peace: For I am with thee, and no man shall set on thee to hurt thee: for I have much people in this city" (Acts 18:9-10). The "much people" were not already Christians, but would become such through Paul's preaching. While in Corinth, Paul wrote 1 and 2 Thessalonians, his first two letters.

Another significant thing took place in Corinth. Some Jews raised a riot and brought Paul before the Roman proconsul Gallio. They accused Paul of preaching against the Jewish law. When Gallio refused to render judgment he gave tacit approval to the Christian movement (18:12-16).

Leaving Corinth, Paul paid a visit to Jerusalem and Antioch. Then at long last he went to Ephesus (19:1). This began his third missionary journey. He spent more than two years in a fruitful ministry there. During this time he was also seeking to raise an offering for the relief of needy

Christians in Jerusalem (1 Cor. 16:1-4; 2 Cor. 8-9). While in Ephesus, Paul wrote 1 Corinthians to deal with problems in the Corinthian church.

Due to a riot in Ephesus he had to leave ahead of schedule. While in Macedonia he wrote 2 Corinthians. From there he went to Corinth for a three-month visit (20:1-3). During this time he wrote Romans and Galatians.

From Corinth, Paul went to Jerusalem. There he was arrested under false accusations. Nevertheless, he spent two years in prison in Caesarea. Finally, failing to receive justice in provincial courts, he exercised his right as a Roman citizen. He appealed to Caesar (25:11-12). Such an appeal could neither be denied nor rescinded. So finally after a stormy voyage and arduous journey, Paul arrived in Rome (Acts 27:1—28:16).

Instead of being put into a prison, Paul was permitted to live for two years "in his own hired house" (28:30). During this time, while waiting to appear before Nero's tribunal, he was chained to a Roman soldier 24 hours each day. But he was allowed to receive all who came to him. It was during this time that he wrote Philippians, Ephesians, Colossians, and Philemon. Had he been free to travel, he probably would have gone to visit these addresses rather than to have written them. How much Christians in every age would have missed without these letters!

Truly God works in all things for good to those who love Him and are the called according to His purpose (Rom. 8:28)!

The Bible:

The New Covenant

(Part 2)

Chapter 7
The Bible: The New Covenant
Part 2

Theologians speak of *progressive revelation.* This does not refer to God's ability to reveal, but to our ability to receive and understand the revelation. Thus we have a clearer revelation of God in John than in Genesis. But it is the same God in both.

If Einstein were teaching a child mathematics, he would not start with his equation on the theory of relativity. He would begin with one plus one equals two—not because that is all the mathematics Einstein knew, but because that is

---

In this chapter, you are reading about the following New Testament books:

Romans	Titus
1 and 2 Corinthians	Philemon
Galatians	Hebrews
Ephesians	James
Philippians	1 and 2 Peter
Colossians	1, 2, and 3 John
1 and 2 Thessalonians	Jude
1 and 2 Timothy	Revelation

To read about the other books in the New Testament, read chapter 6.

all that the child can receive at that stage of development. It is necessary that the child know that simple equation before proceeding through higher and more complex phases of mathematics. Eventually the great teacher will lead his pupil to cope with equations related to relativity and splitting the atom. That is progressive teaching of mathematics.

This enables us to comprehend God's progressive revelation. God reveals Himself through nature, His mighty works, the human conscience, and through chosen human vessels empowered by the Holy Spirit. He reveals Himself through His written Word. You need only to read the Old Testament to comprehend the progressive nature of His revelation under the old covenant.

But God's full, complete revelation is in His Son Jesus Christ. Jesus said, "I and my Father are one" (John 10:30). The night before His death He said to His apostles, "He that hath seen me hath seen the Father" (John 14:9). For 3½ years He had taught them. Also He had shown them the works of the Father. Following the institution of the Lord's Supper He taught them intensely (John 14—16). In John 14:26 Jesus said that after His return to the Father the Holy Spirit will come to teach them all things. And in John 16:12 He said, "I have yet many things to say unto you, but ye cannot bear them now."

The brief teaching periods following Jesus' resurrection hardly satisfy the implication of teachings yet to come. Apparently Jesus referred to the teachings and writings of Spirit-led men

The Temple

as seen in the remaining books of the New Testament—the Epistles and Revelation. The revelation of God was complete in Jesus Christ. There remained the interpretation of His revelation. In the remainder of this chapter we will examine briefly the rest of the books of the New Testament. These books are not chronologically arranged in the Bible. But we will treat them in the order in which they appear in it.

Romans

In the seminary A. T. Robertson was fond of telling about a trial lawyer in Louisville, Kentucky. Having finished preparation for a court case, just prior to going into court he would lie on a couch while his secretary read to him the book of Romans. He said that it sharpened his argumentative powers. And well he might do so. For Romans is the most logical presentation of the gospel on record.

Paul planned a preaching trip to Spain. On his way he would visit the church in Rome (Rom. 15:23-24). He had many friends in Rome whom he had known elsewhere (Rom 16). But for the most part the saints in Rome had never heard him preach. So he wrote this letter setting forth the gospel as he preached it.

Because of what God in Christ had done for him, Paul felt obligated to share the gospel with the whole world (1:14-15). He had never been disappointed with the gospel (1:16). Wherever proclaimed, it bore a harvest of souls.

Paul described the gospel as twofold in nature. It reveals God's righteousness or saving work for those who believe in His Son. But it also reveals His wrath against all ungodliness and unrighteousness and those who practice them (1:17-18). No one can excuse himself on the basis of ignorance about God who has revealed Himself (1:19-20).

Romans 1:21-32 pictures the terrible nature of sin. Writing in Corinth, Paul saw it there. Romans 2—3 shows how both Jew and Gentile (pagans) are guilty before God and hopeless apart from God's redemptive work in Christ. In Romans 4 Paul uses Abraham as an example that we can only be saved by faith apart from works. (See also chapter 5.) Though not saved by works, Christians should dedicate themselves to God's service (Rom. 6). And even Christians must continue to war against temptation (Rom. 7). Romans 8 is Paul's great chapter on the normal working of the Holy Spirit in the life of the Christian. And in Romans 9—11 the apostle treats the problem of both Jew and Gentile in God's redemptive purpose.

Paul's normal pattern was, first, to expound doctrine, and, then, to apply it to Christian living (Rom. 12—15). Romans 15:24-32 deals with the apostle's future plans. Chapter 16 is related to personal matters.

1 and 2 Corinthians

If a pastor wants to deal with most every problem in a church, let him preach through these two epistles. At the same time, in dealing with these problems Paul touches upon some of the great themes of the Christian faith: the cross, the resurrection, stewardship, and Christian love.

While in Ephesus, Paul learned of these problems. So he wrote 1 Corinthians. Then from Macedonia he wrote 2 Corinthians. The latter was written primarily to deal with those who still opposed Paul and to spur the church to fulfill its agreement to participate in the relief offering for Jerusalem Christians.

A suggestion made by G. Campbell Morgan[1] fits both letters. He sees 1 Corinthians 1:9 and 15:58 as parentheses enclosing all the problems in the letter. "God is faithful . . . Therefore . . . be ye stedfast, unmoveable, always abounding in the work of the Lord, forasmuch as ye know that your labour is not in vain in the Lord."

Galatians

Galatians may well be called a "Mini-Romans." Both letters deal with justification by faith. Apparently both were written from Corinth during Paul's third missionary journey. It is possible that the apostle wrote Galatians, and then Romans. There is a calmer, more logical style in Romans. Galatians was written with a "red-hot pen."

Word reached Paul that some Judaizers were disturbing the largely Gentile churches in Galatia. The strong language in Galatians 1:6-9 indicates the tone of the letter. "Accursed" translates "anathema," something so vile that its destruction brings glory to God. Galatians 1 also contains Paul's version of the Jerusalem Conference (Acts 15).

Ephesians

Ephesians is a circular letter sent to the churches of the Roman province of Asia. It was written from Rome during Paul's first Roman imprisonment. He was awaiting his appearance before Caesar's tribunal, not knowing if he would be set free or put to death. Since he was the apostle to the Gentiles, we may well imagine his wondering what would happen to the cause of Christ should he be put to death. Then he thought of the churches he and others had established. In them lay the future of God's redemptive purpose. So to such he wrote this letter, the cream of his theological thought.

Actually Ephesians is Paul's treatment of the doctrine of election. "Hath chosen" (1:4, KJV) renders a Greek word which comes into English as "elected." This does not mean that God elected certain people to be saved to the neglect of all others. God's purpose is to save as many, not as few, as He can.

The fact is that God in His sovereignty elected a *plan* of salvation (Eph. 1—2) and a *people* to propagate the plan (Eph. 3—6). Man in his free will can choose to accept or reject them. God elected "in Christ." "In love" (v. 4, KJV) probably should be a part of verse 5. Whatever God did, He did it in love.

"Having predestinated" (v. 5) renders a Greek verb which means to set a boundary beforehand. It is like building a fence about a piece of land. The fence is Christ. In His sovereign will God in eternity said that all "in Christ" will be saved. All outside of Christ will be lost. In Ephesians 1:3-11 Paul uses "in Christ" or its equivalent 10 times.

But in his free will man can choose to be in Christ or outside of Christ. He is, however, responsible for his choice. "After that ye believed" expresses man's free will (1:13). Once having believed in Christ a person is both saved and safe (1:13b-14).

Ephesians 2 shows how this plan works. The things which separated Jew and Gentile are removed in Christ. In fact, in Christ God is creating out of Jews and Gentiles a new order of mankind—Christians—who have direct, equal access to God (2:11-15).

Ephesians 3—6 deals with the people who are to propagate the plan of salvation. These Paul describes as the "church," the body of Christ composed of all the redeemed of all the ages. We are to live in accord with our calling as children of God (4:1). In 6:10-20 the apostle pictures Christians as soldiers of Christ at war with Satan. In this description he likens the equipment worn by the soldier to whom he was chained. It includes all of a soldier's battle gear except greaves (shin guards) and a spear. These would not be needed by a soldier on guard duty. Note that Paul lists no armor to protect the soldier's back. A Roman soldier was never to turn his back to the enemy. And neither should we. The only offensive weapon is the sword of the Spirit, God's word.

Philippians

No church was dearer to Paul's heart than the one in Philippi. And they returned that love, as seen in the repeated monetary gifts they sent to him. It was such a gift that prompted this letter (4:10-19). No other church is mentioned as doing this.

In his letter Paul reported his condition. The gospel was still winning victories in Rome (1:17-19).

Paul was still awaiting his appearance before Caesar. Whatever the verdict, life or death, he was ready for it (1:19-25).

Paul had every reason to complain over what had happened to him. But the keynote of this epistle is joy.

Colossians

While under house arrest in Rome, Paul received word that the Gnostics (see John's Gospel, chapter 6) were disturbing the church in Colossae. Unable to go there, he wrote this letter in which he exalts Jesus Christ as "the image [exact manifestation] of the invisible God, the Lord of all creation" (1:15). "Firstborn" doesn't mean that Christ was a created being and not eternal in nature, the very thing Paul denies. The word here means prior being with the sense of "Lordship." Gerhard Kittel so translates it here.[2]

Verse 17 reads, literally, "And he is before every single thing in the universe, and in him the universe as a whole holds together." We live in a Christ-centered universe. Colossians 2:9 is one of the greatest statements of the full deity of Jesus. We will ever be in debt to Paul.

1 and 2 Thessalonians

In all probability these were Paul's first and second letters, both written from Corinth. Some see Galatians as his first letter, written from Antioch shortly after the Jerusalem Conference in A.D. 49. But it seems more likely that Galatians was written just before Romans during Paul's three-month visit to Corinth near the end of his third missionary journey (Acts 20:3).

While in Thessalonica during his second missionary journey Paul had taught about Jesus' second coming. Apparently after he left Thessalonica someone else had taught the Thessalonian Christians in such a manner as to confuse them on this matter.

In the meantime some of the Christians in Thessalonica had died. The living were concerned that at the Lord's return He would take them to heaven, leaving their dead loved ones behind. So Paul wrote to assure them that their dead loved ones would be raised and with them be taken to heaven (4:13-18).

However, Paul's first letter did not fully solve the problem. So he wrote 2 Thessalonians, in which he dealt further with the matter (2:1-17). He showed that certain things must take place before the Lord's return. This is a difficult passage to interpret.

1 and 2 Timothy, Titus

These are known as the pastoral epistles. Though not related in Acts we assume from these epistles that Paul was acquitted in his appearance before Caesar's tribunal. From the church fathers we learn that he went to Spain.

Apparently from there he returned east across the Mediterranean. At Crete he left Titus to supervise the work there (Titus 1:5). Then he returned to Ephesus. From there he went to Macedonia, leaving Timothy in Ephesus (1 Tim. 1:3).

From Macedonia Paul wrote 1 Timothy, rehearsing his own experience in the Lord and giving instructions to Timothy relative to the work in Ephesus. Also he wrote to encourage Titus in Crete.

Later Paul was arrested, taken to Rome, and condemned to death. From a dungeon he wrote 2 Timothy. Apparently uncertain as to the time of his execution, he urges Timothy to be faithful in the work and to come to him. Paul has been forsaken by all except Luke (2 Tim. 4:9-11). Regardless of what happens to him, Paul is confident about his future in the Lord (2 Tim. 4:6-8).

The Bible does not record Paul's death. But tradition says that he was beheaded outside Rome. Thus died the greatest interpreter and servant of Christ.

Philemon

This shortest of all Paul's epistles is a gem in tactful dealing with a delicate subject. Onesimus, a slave of Philemon, ran away to Rome. There he came into contact with Paul. Paul led him to Christ and with this letter sent Onesimus back to Philemon in Colossae. He urges Philemon to receive him, not as a slave but as a Christian brother. He even signs a promissory note (vv. 18-19) that he will pay his friend Philemon any damages caused by Onesimus. But note in verse 19b Paul's reminder that, since Paul led Philemon to Christ, he owes himself to Paul. In effect, Paul reminds Philemon that he is a *piker* if he makes him pay the note.

Philemon is a masterpiece in diplomacy. Outside of the Gospels, it has done more than any other document to end human slavery.

Hebrews

This epistle is a complex book. Who was its author? To whom was it written? What was the author's purpose in writing?

Various possible authors have been suggested: Paul, Apollos, Barnabas, Priscilla. These and others have been suggested. Since the author refers to himself with a masculine pronoun, that seems to rule out Priscilla. "Law" in Hebrews refers to ceremonial law. In his writings Paul deals with law other than ceremonial law. So it is unlikely that Paul wrote it.

The author seems to be of the Alexandrian school of thought. This school used the allegorical method of interpretation. This seems to be the method used by the author of Hebrews. This method could fit either Apollos or Barnabas. Martin Luther and A. T. Robertson suggest Apollos as the author. However, the letter is built around five exhortations (2:1-3; 3:7-19; 6:1-6; 10:19-30; 12:1-15). Barnabas means "son of exhortation" (*bar,* son, *nabas,* exhortation; Acts 4:36, "consolation" may also read "exhortation"). For this reason I opt for Barnabas as the author. The church father Origen says of the author that "only God knows" who he was. One must decide for himself.

The oldest Greek manuscripts of Hebrews simply read "To Hebrews." In all likelihood the addresses were a congregation of Hebrew Christians somewhere in the Roman empire. It is uncertain whether the letter was written from Rome to a congregation elsewhere or written elsewhere to a congregation in Rome (13:24). "They of Italy" could refer to people living in Italy or to those from Italy living elsewhere. I opt for the former view.

Some interpreters see the author's purpose as warning Jews not to stop short of receiving Christ. But the author addresses them in terms which suggest that they are already Christians (3:1). Others see the letter as addressed to Hebrew Christians warning them not to turn from Christ and thus lose their salvation. I see the warning being against failure to develop and serve in God's world mission of redemption, thus losing their opportunity in God's service.

My view is that the author is giving an allegorical interpretation of the Exodus epic. It centers in Numbers 13—14 where Israel rebelled at Kadesh-barnea. She refused to enter the land of Canaan, the land from which Israel was to carry out her covenant to be a priest-nation to the pagan world endeavoring to bring it to worship and serve Jehovah. That generation did not lose its redemption from Egyptian bondage. Rather it wandered in the desert wilderness until all of those 20 years and older died in the wilderness. They lost their opportunity!

This corresponds to Christians who are a covenant people (Jer. 31:31-34; Heb. 8). If they fail to develop and serve in God's redemptive mission, they too will lose their opportunity (Heb. 5:11-14).

The theme of Hebrews is not "Don't go back" into an unredeemed state. It is "Let us go on unto perfection" (Heb. 6:1) or the fulfillment of their purpose of being.

James

The author of this letter is a half-brother to Jesus. But being no "name-dropper," he makes no mention of that fact. He simply calls himself "a servant [bondslave] of God and of the Lord Jesus Christ." (1:1).

James was probably the first book in the New Testament to be written. Since he makes no reference to the Jerusalem Conference (Acts 15, A.D. 49), it could have been written as early as A.D. 48. James was the pastor of the Jerusalem church.

This is the most Hebraic book in the New Testament. Note that "assembly" (2:2) renders the word for "synagogue." Also it is the most practical book in the New Testament, showing how Christian faith should produce good works in daily living.

Some interpreters see a conflict between James and Paul with respect to works and salvation (2:17-26). However, they are saying the same thing, only from different perspectives. James says that the kind of faith that saves also produces good works. Paul says we are saved by grace through faith "unto good works" (Eph. 2:8-10).

1 and 2 Peter

Peter was the apostle to the Jews (Gal. 2:9). His former epistle is addressed to the "Dispersion" ("scattered," v. 1). This word was used of Jews living outside Palestine. He uses it to denote Jewish Christians who lived outside that land.

Apparently it was during a time of religious persecution. "Temptations" may read "trials" (1:6-7). So Peter wrote to encourage Christians in hard times. They have been redeemed by the blood of Christ (1:18-20). And they are committed to proclaim the gospel (1:22-25).

In chapter 2 (vv. 1-10) Peter shows that his readers, along with all believers, are the true Israel, God's covenant people to declare the gospel to all the world. The remainder of the epistle deals with Christian living on the part of Peter's readers. They are ever to be an example in public and personal life of what Christ does to one who submits to Him (3:15-17). If they suffer at the hands of others it should not be as criminals but as Christians (5:15-16).

Of interest is the fact that 3:20-21 does not teach baptismal regeneration. Noah and his family were not saved by being in the water. They were saved through the flood by being in the ark, a type of Christ. "Baptism" translates *baptisma*. It does not refer to the act of baptism, but to the meaning in the act—death, burial, and resurrection—what Jesus did for our salvation. It also denotes what happens to us when we believe in Jesus—we die to the old life, it is buried, and we are raised to walk in newness of life. This word, *baptisma,* is not found in any Greek writing other than the New Testament and later ecclesiastical writings. It seems that the Holy Spirit coined this word to express the meaning in the act of baptism. Rather than being a saving ordinance, it symbolizes what is involved in the saving experience.

Second Peter (see 3:1) reminds the readers of their initial experience in Christ, warns against false prophets and sins of the flesh (2:1-22). Also Peter warns against those who will scoff at the idea of Christ's second coming, due to its delay. But he reminds his readers that time is no element with God (3:1-8). He assures them that Christ will return and calls upon them to consider their life-style in light of the "blessed hope" (Titus 2:13).

The Johannine Epistles

In many ways 1 John reminds us of John's Gospel (1 John 1:1-3). It was written to combat Gnosticism. Some see 1 John 3:9 to teach sinless perfection. But "commit" is a present tense of repeated action. It does not deny that Christians will commit an occasional sin (1 John 1:8—2:2). Rather, Christians are not to make sinful living their on-going life-style.

Also John calls upon us to judge between the spirits whether the Spirit (spirit) be of God (4:1). Not every spiritual phenomenon is of the Holy Spirit. For the spirit of Satan is also at work in the world.

Furthermore, John sounds the note that "God is love" (4:8). For this reason we should love one another.

Second John also warns against "deceivers" that are in the world (v. 7). A day such as ours needs this message.

Among other notes sounded in 3 John is the condemnation of "bossism" in a New Testament church. It is not clear whether Diotrephes is a pastor or a layman. But the message is the same in either case.

Jude

Like James, Jude was also a half-brother of Jesus. But he also identifies himself as "the servant of Jesus Christ, and brother of James" (v. 1). Warning against false teachers (v. 4), he describes such in vivid and picturesque language.

Revelation

This book was written by John while in exile on the isle of Patmos. It is addressed to seven churches in the Roman province of Asia (1:11).

"Revelation" translates *apokalupsis* (apocalypse). It means an unveiling. Apocalyptic language was a code language used by Jews to communicate with one another during times of persecution. It made use of ancient numerology as well as disturbances in natures. This code was understood by Jews, but was unknown to their enemies.

Is this book to be interpreted literally or symbolically? In 1:1 "signified" means to show in signs or symbols. Thus I believe that the author intended the book to be symbolic. The visions of Revelation, however, are interpreted in a variety of ways by Bible-believing Christians. Reasonably, I feel that it is presented as a drama—the drama of the sovereignty of God in Christ. Its overriding theme is the victory of Christ over all that/who oppose Him.

The historical setting is persecution of the Christians by the Roman emperor Domitian (A.D. 81-96). Any interpretation of Revelation must give courage to the Christians of that era. But it also declares principles which apply in any age. Evil forces may seem to be triumphant at a given time. But the final victory belongs to Christ and His people. And this is a proper conclusion for the Bible.

The Bible:

The Canon of Scripture

Chapter 8
The Bible: The Canon of Scripture

With the sixty-six books having been written by so many people in far-flung places and over so many centuries, how did they become one book, the Bible? It is a long, interesting story. In our limited space we can only present a sketch of it.[1] Suffice it to say that as the Holy Spirit inspired the writers, so we may see His hand in the forming of the canon of the Scriptures.

The Meaning of "Canon"

The word "canon" is a transliteration of the Greek *kanon*, which, in turn, probably came from the Hebrew *kaneh*. The Hebrew word means a reed or measuring rod. From this comes the idea of a rule. It came to be used of a measurement of faith.

"Canon" is now used of a body of sacred writings, hence, the Bible. In the New Testament the Greek word is found in 2 Corinthians 10:13-16 and Galatians 6:16 where it is translated as "rule" (KJV). But it was in the fourth century A.D. that it is found in its present sense. This was at the Council of Laodicea in A.D. 363. So in this sense, the word "canon" had a Christian origin.

The question naturally comes as to who had the authority to decide which writings should be in the canon of Scripture. We have already noted the guidance of the Holy Spirit. But while the forming of the canon had a divine side, it also had a human side, just as did the inspiration and original writing of the books.

One determining factor was the name related to a writing, such as Moses, Isaiah, Paul, and the like. Another was the nature of the writings themselves. There were many writings not included in the canon. While they are important in their own way, such as information, they did/do not speak to the spiritual needs of people. So through a process of elimination, certain writings were chosen. Samuel Taylor Coleridge has been quoted as saying, "I know the Bible is inspired because it finds me at a greater depth of my being than any other book." The third determining factor grew out of the second, the use of the writings in public worship. Gradually certain ones came to be used, for they were found to contain the spiritual message of God to the people's hearts.

Eventually, conferences were held in which the canon of each Testament was approved. However, they only affirmed what had already been accepted by the people who had accepted certain books as being inspired of God. Thus the process of determining the canon did not work from the top down to the people. The opposite was true. It worked from the bottom up as the Holy Spirit moved in the hearts of the people of God.

The Old Testament Canon

It is not surprising that the Bible itself does not tell how the canon of Scripture was formed. The writers were unaware of the fact that they were writing books for what we call the Bible. However, certain clues are available in how the people regarded these writings.

Old Testament Witness

The Old Testament contains passages which show how carefully certain portions were preserved. For instance, Exodus 40:20 says that Moses put the "testimony" (the stones containing Ten Commandments) in the Ark of the Covenant. Deuteronomy 31:24-26 relates that when Moses finished writing the law in a book, he commanded the Levites to put the book "in the side of the ark of the covenant of the Lord your God, that it may be there for a witness against thee" (Deut. 31:26). This suggests that this book was regarded as a rule of faith which was binding upon the Israelites. In 1 Kings 8:9 only the two tables of stones were in the ark when Solomon moved it into the Temple (see 2 Kings 11:12).

As a part of Josiah's religious reforms he had the Temple renovated. In the process they found "the book of the law" (Deuteronomy). When it was read to Josiah, he learned how the people had neglected the worship prescribed in the law. They recognized that it contained the words of God and used it in reestablishing worship of Him (2 Kings 22:8—23:3). This shows that they recognized the binding nature of this book as a rule of faith.

One of the most significant passages in this regard is Nehemiah 8:1—9:3. When the walls of Jerusalem had been rebuilt, the people had a renewal of the covenant with God. Day by day the people stood and heard Ezra read from "the book of the law of Moses" (8:1).

Now these and other examples do not necessarily refer to the canon of Scripture. But they do show the care given to preserving the law and regarded it as a divine rule of faith and practice.

Divisions of the Old Testament

Early in their history, the Jews divided their Scriptures into three categories: the Law, the Prophets, and the Writings (see Luke 24:44). The Law or *Troah* included the five books of Moses (Gen.-Deut.).

According to Robinson the Prophets included "the four so-called Former Prophets, Josh, Jgs, 1 and 2 S, counted as one book, 1 and 2 K, also counted as one book; and the four so-called Latter Prophets, Isa, Jer, Ezk, and the Twelve Minor Prophets, counted as one book; a total of 8 books. The . . . Writings were 11 in all, including Ps, Prov, and Job, the five . . . Rolls (Cant [Songs of Solomon], Ruth, Lam, Eccl, Est), Dnl, Ezra-Neh, counted as one book, and 1 and 2 Ch, also counted as one book; in all 24 books, exactly the same as those of the Protestant canon."[2] (Of course, when you divide those counted as one book this number is thirty-seven.) According to Robinson, "This was the original count of the Jews as far as we can trace it back."[3] Jerome

(Vulgate) agreed with this figure.

However, it should be noted that this canonization did not happen immediately. It developed gradually as the need for authoritative writings became more acute. The books of Law were the first to be canonized. Later this happened to the prophets, and finally to the Writings.

The greatest pressure for a canon of Old Testament Scripture came following the fall of Jerusalem and the temple in 587 B.C. The exile called for a rallying point. This was found in a body of authoritative Scripture. Thus it was that when Ezra returned to Jerusalem he brought a book of the Law which was later read to the people in a covenant renewal.

This process was also hastened by later Greek efforts to convert the Jews to Greek culture and religion. This was especially during the reign of Antiochus Epiphanes in the Seleucid kingdom whose capital was Antioch in Syria (175-164 B.C.).

The Septuagint

When Alexander the Great founded Alexandria, Egypt, he did so with a colony of Jews. In time it became a great center of learning. Also in time many of the Jews of Alexandria were unable to read Hebrew. Therefore a request was sent to the high priest in Jerusalem for scholars to be sent to Alexandria to translate the Hebrew Scriptures into Greek. This work is called the Septuagint.

"Septuagint comes from the Greek word for "seventy." According to tradition seventy rabbis, working independently, produced the translation in seventy days. It produced seventy identical Greek texts! Whatever the process, they produced a monumental text from which New Testament writers nearly always quoted when citing the Old Testament. They did so because they understood and wrote Greek rather than Hebrew.

When the Alexandrian canon was established, they also included the fourteen books of the Apocrypha which means "hidden," reflecting the anonymous character of these books. The Roman Catholics include these in their Bible. However, the Protestant canon followed the Hebrew canon and so omitted them. As previously noted, the Apocrypha is valuable as information about the time in which its books were written (about 200 B.C.-A.D. 100). But they lack the spiritual quality of Scripture.

The Councils of Jamnia

Jamnia was located not many miles south of Joppa (south of modern Tel Aviv) on the Mediterranean coast. Two councils of rabbis were held there in A.D. 90 and 118. Accurate records of these councils have not been preserved. But it is generally agreed by scholars that a century-old conflict between the rival schools of Hillel and Shammai was settled.

The Old Testament canon of 39 books as we know them was fixed. This council of itself did not set the canon. What they did was to ratify what was already generally accepted. Thus, as previously noted, the Holy Spirit worked, not from the top down, but from the bottom up.

The New Testament Canon

When the New Testament speaks of "the scriptures," it usually refers to the Old Testament. It was at least 19 years after Jesus' resurrection before the first part of the New Testament was written. And, as far as we know, no writer of the New Testament was aware of the fact that he was writing what would become a part of the Bible.

In his treatment of the canon of Scripture, J. S. Riggs makes three divisions: From the Apostles to A.D. 170; the period from A.D. 170 to 220; the third and fourth centuries.

Apostles to A.D. 170

By the end of the first century A.D. all the New Testament writings were in existence. As J. S. Riggs suggests, each of these writings was probably a treasure of widely separated churches. With the death of the apostles and other authors, they assumed even greater importance. These documents no doubt were read repeatedly in worship services.

In time, churches began to exchange copies of these writings. Colossians 4:16 shows an example of this even in Paul's lifetime. The letter "from Laodicea" probably refers to Ephesians. In A.D. 110 Polycarp wrote to the Philippians, "I have received letters from you and from Ignatius. You recommended me to send yours to Syria; I shall do so either personally or by some other means. In return I send you the letter of Ignatius as well as others which I have in my hands and for which you made request. I add them to the present one; they will serve to edify your faith and perseverance."

In all likelihood by this time the four Gospels had been gathered together as a unit. The oldest example of Scripture to be found thus far is a portion of John's Gospel in a Chester Beatty papyrus now in the John Rylands Library in Manchester, England. Papyrologists agree that it should not be dated later than the first quarter of the second century A.D. Some date it in the last quarter of the second century A.D. This gives us some idea as to the wide circulation of Christian writings at so early a date.

Of course this is a far cry from canonization. But it does show the esteem with which these documents were held.

Furthermore, the early church fathers reflect their esteem and reliance upon the first century writings. For instance, in A.D. 95 Clement of Rome wrote a letter to the Corinthian church. In it he gives a free rendering of passages in Matthew and Luke. He shows the influence upon him of Romans and Hebrews. Also he shows acquaintance with 1 Timothy, Titus, Ephesians, and 1 Peter.

A.D. 170-220

A step toward the forming of the New Testament canon is found in the apologists against a hostile civil government and heretics. Of these Justin Martyr is typical. In his apologies he speaks of the "Memoirs of the Apostles, called Gospels." He says that on Sundays they were read along with the prophets, thus placing them on an equality with the Old Testament prophets. That he had in mind the four Gospels is evident in the fact that Tatian, his pupil, made a harmony of the four Gospels.

Irenaeus was a pupil of Polycarp who, in turn, was one of the Apostle John's disciples. In his defense of the Christian faith he quotes from the four Gospels, Acts, the Pauline epistles, several of the general epistles and the Revelation; he regarded all these as inspired Scripture. Tertullian in North Africa does virtually the same. Clement of Alexandria quotes from the Gospels as Scripture. Riggs says, "By the end of the 2d cent. the canon of the Gospels was settled. The same is true also of the Pauline epistles."[4] He also notes that the title "New Testament" is first used by an unknown writer about A.D. 193. After this it occurs often in Origen and later writers.

The Muratorian Canon

This is a fragment found in 1740 by Muratori, librarian of Milan, Italy, from whom it gets its name. It belongs to the second century A.D. Its value in the study of the canon is that it contains the four Gospels, Acts, the Pauline epistles, Revelation, 1 and 2 John, and Jude.

This shows the state of the New Testament canon at the close of the second century A.D. Other books were still unsettled. The Palestinian and Syrian churches rejected the Revelation for a long period. The acceptance of the remaining books came in the third and fourth centuries A.D.

Third and Fourth Centuries

The most notable name in the third century was Origen of Alexandria. As an authority on the Scriptures he was highly regarded in various other centers of learning.

Origen accepted the Gospels, Acts, the Pauline epistles, and Revelation. Though he said that "God alone knows who wrote" Hebrews, he also accepts this book. He also accepted Jude. But he was not certain about 2 Peter, 2 and 3 John.

In the early part of the fourth century Eusebius (A.D. 270-340), bishop of Caesarea before A.D. 315, gave the state of the canon in his time. He gave two categories: the undisputed books and the disputed ones. In the former he placed the Gospels, Acts, the Pauline epistles, and Hebrews. The latter, which had received only partial recognition, included James, Jude, 2 Peter, and 2 John. He was not certain about Revelation. He does not reflect much advance over the third century.

Riggs noted that the spread of Christianity by the time of the emperor Constantine led him to request Eusebius to prepare "fifty copies of the Divine Scriptures." This provided a standard which "in time gave recognition to all doubtful books."

In A.D. 397 the Council of Carthage decreed "that aside from the canonical Scriptures nothing is to be read in church under the name of Divine Scriptures."

In concluding this rather tedious discussion of the formation of the canon, we recognize the human element involved. Conscientious men debated issues. But we may rest assured that the Holy Spirit guided and overruled the differences of men. We may in confidence accept and believe that what we call the "Holy Bible" in indeed the sure Word of God.

9

The Bible:

The Book
for the
People

Chapter 9
The Bible: The Book for the People

When you hold in your hand a copy of the Bible, you are holding a treasure of the ages. You not only hold a volume of divinely inspired writings; it is also the product of almost endless labor of an innumerable host of devoted people.

We tend to take the Bible for granted. But if any other book had undergone the efforts to destroy it as has the Bible, it would have disappeared centuries ago. However, the Bible has withstood them all. It has come to us floating on a river of martyrs' blood. You can almost smell the smoke of martyrs' fires on its pages. But the Holy Spirit who inspired it through dedicated people has preserved it so that the circulation of the Bible today exceeds that of any other book.

Language of the People

The original manuscripts were written in the language of the contemporary people. With the exception of a few isolated cases, the Old Testament was written in Hebrew. The New Testament was written in Greek.

Through the years the Greek scholars noticed the difference between the Greek of the New Testament and that of Greek classical writings, the language of the ancient scholars. They spoke of classical Greek and New Testament Greek. One scholar called the latter "the language of the Holy Ghost," as if the Holy Spirit had invented this special Greek to be used in writing the New Testament.

However, with discovery of the papyri this concept has radically changed. Thanks to Adolf Deissmann, we now know that the New Testament Greek was the everyday common Greek of the people. Thus it is called *Koine* or common Greek. So we know that the Bible originally was written in the language of the people.

The oldest complete Hebrew text dates from A.D. 1008. The discovery of the Dead Sea scrolls uncovered much valuable textual materials, including a complete copy of the prophecy of Isaiah which antedates the birth of Christ. Among other things, the discovery has served to show the accuracy of the A.D. text.

Any classical Greek scholar is fortunate to have as many as fifteen manuscripts of a given Greek classic. But there are thousands of available manuscripts or fragments of the Greek New Testament either in part or in whole. An axiom of manuscript study is that, with a few exceptions, the older the manuscript the more accurate it is. Following this axiom, New Testament scholars have practically arrived at the wording of the original manuscripts.

Variety of Translations

Even before the New Testament era the Hebrew scriptures had been translated into other languages. The Septuagint is the best known. But other translations had been made to enable Jews throughout the Roman world to read their Scriptures in the languages spoken by them.

The same need led to many translations of the entire Bible, including the New Testament. As the gospel spread, so the translations followed. For the people of the West and Africa, Latin was used. In Syria, Syriac was used. For the Egyptians, it was Coptic. Later came Armenian, Ethopic, Arabic, and Georgian. In the fourth century, the Pope commissioned Jerome, a Latin Bible scholar, to revise the earlier Latin version in order to provide a standard translation. For nearly fifteen hundred years, Jerome's Vulgate, meaning "common" or vernacular," was the official Bible for the Roman Church.

However, in time the situation was such that only the highly educated could read Latin, so the Bible was largely lost from the masses of people. Furthermore, the Roman Catholic Church held that only priests could interpret the Bible.

Struggle for Survivial

The Protestant Reformation set in motion a chain of events designed to restore the Bible to the people. With the Latin Vulgate as the standard Bible, knowledge of Greek largely was lost. Someone said that during the Renaissance (14-15 centuries) Greece rose from the grave with the Greek New Testament in her hands. This, plus the invention of the printing press, stimulated great interest in the translation and distribution of the scriptures.

John Wycliffe made the first complete translation from the Latin into the English of his day. This was done in the face of opposition from the constituted religious and civil authorities. But so popular was his work that men paid a load of hay for the privilege of reading it for one hour.

After his death Wycliffe was denounced by the Archbishop of Canterbury as "that pestilent wretch of damnable memory, son of that old sea serpent, yea the forerunner and disciple of the antichrist, who as the complement of his wickedness, invented a new translation of the Scriptures into his mother tongue." One monk called Wycliffe "the organ of the devil, the enemy of the Church, the idol of heretics, the image of hypocrites, the restorer of schism, the storehouse of lies, the sink of flattery." (Both forgot that Jerome's Vulgate which they used was a translation of Greek into the "mother tongue," Latin.) In A.D. 1415 the Council of Constance condemned his writings and his bones to the flames.

In 1516 Erasmus published his Greek New Testament. He longed "for the day when the husbandman shall sing to himself portions of the Scriptures as he follows the plough, when the weaver shall hum them to the tune of his shuttle, when the traveler shall while away with their stories the weariness of his journey." Erasmus' great desire took root in the soul of his pupil William Tyndale.

Tyndale translated the Scriptures from Greek into English. Due to opposition in England, in 1524 he fled to Germany. Under the protection of Martin Luther he continued his work. But even there he encountered opposition. So he fled from

Cologne to Worms. There he completed translating and printing of the first translation into English of the Greek New Testament.

It is said that he finished setting his type late one afternoon. During the night vandals destroyed the type. He patiently resumed his task, finishing it by the end of 1525.

The following year he smuggled Bibles into England in sacks of flour. The people received them joyfully. But the bishops sent agents to purchase and destroy them. However, the Bibles continued to come so that England was flooded with copies of the New Testament in English.

Finally, Tyndale was arrested, and on October 6, 1536, he was strangled and burned. His dying prayer was, "Lord, open the King of England's eyes." His prayer was answered with the publication of the King James Version of the Bible in 1611.

These incidents merely illustrate the struggle to place the Bible in the hands of the people. The authoritative Church and State did all they could to prevent it. But the Bible emerged from the struggle victorious. It was God's power through dedicated servants empowered by the Holy Spirit.

Other English Versions

The first complete English Bible to be printed came from the press in 1535. It was the work of Myles Coverdale, but most of the material came from Tyndale's translation. Thomas Cromwell, vicegerent of King Henry VIII, requested that Coverdale prepare what would be known as an authorized Bible. In 1539 Coverdale issued a revised edition of his and other English translations. Because of the large pages it was known as the "Great Bible." The psalms from the Great Bible are still in use in the Book of Common Prayer of the Church of England.

During the reign of Queen Mary, Catholic daughter of Henry VIII, some Protestants were living in exile in Geneva, Switzerland. In 1560 they published a Bible in English. Thus it was called the Geneva Bible. It proved to be very popular in England. Between 1560 and 1630 about two hundred editions were printed.

The popularity of the Geneva Bible resulted in the publishing of 1568 of another known as the Bishops' Bible. The bishops of the Church of England felt that the Geneva Bible was not suited to use in their services. The Bishops' Bible was published to counteract the influence of the Geneva Bible. It was in large measure a revision of the Great Bible.

It should be noted also that during this period of Reformation in England a Roman Catholic Bible also was published in English. As the Geneva Bible was published by Protestants exiled in Geneva, so this Catholic Bible was published by Roman Catholic scholars exiled in France. (These two exiled groups reflect the struggle in England as to whether Protestants or Catholics would rule in that land.)

The New Testament was done in Rheims, France, in 1582. Thus it is known as the Rheims Version. The Old Testament was published in 1609-1610 at Douai, using the Vulgate. It was later revised and combined with the Rheims New Testament to form the Douai Version. In 1810 it became the approved English version from Roman Catholics in America.

King James Version

Because this is the last and best of the English translations to appear in the Reformation period, it seems wise to give it a more detailed treatment. It seems safe to say that the King James Version has affected Protestant Christianity more than any other, and, perhaps, more than all others combined.

By the beginning of the seventeenth century there was much interest in the need for a standard readable, vernacular Bible. So King James I caused to be assembled a group of fifty scholars who began their work in 1604. These scholars were divided into six groups. Three groups worked on the Old Testament, two on the New Testament, and one on the Apocrypha. Within each group individual assignments were made. When these assignments were completed they were reviewed by the entire group. Suggestions were requested from the other groups. Comparisons with previous versions were made. The finished version came out in 1611. Between that time and 1769 the King James Version went through various revisions to reach its final form. For many English-speaking Christians during the past centuries it has been "The Holy Bible."

Modern Translations

Translations have originated during various periods in history, each trying to make God's Word available in the language most familiar to the people of its generation. Some of the major translations and their publication dates include:

King James 1611
American Standard 1901
Revised Standard 1952
New English 1970
New American Standard 1971
The Living Bible 1971
Today's English Bible 1976
New International Version 1978
New King James 1982
Revised English Bible 1989
New Revised Standard 1990

Translations have also come from different groups whose purposes for doing a particular translation are different. For example, the *New American Standard* originated with the Lockman Foundation, a private group of conservative, evangelical Christians dedicated to distributing God's Word to as many people as possible. Similarly, the *New International Version* comes from the International Bible Society, and *Today's English Version* is from the American Bible Society. The *Revised Standard Version* and the *New Revised Standard Version* are products of an organization of mainline Protestant churches, while the *Revised English Bible* comes from churches in England. *The Living Bible*, a paraphrase, is the work of only one person, Ken Taylor. The *New King James Version* is the product of a publishing house—Thomas Nelson.

Translations are directed to different audiences. Originally, the *New Century Version* and *The Living Bible* were for children. The *New American Bible* was for Catholics and the *New*

Jewish translation for Jews. The *New American Standard* and the *New International Version* developed from the concerns of conservative, evangelical Christians. *Today's English Version* came from a Bible society desiring to make God's Word more easily understood among the people of the world to whom the society distributes Scriptures.

From time to time there have been individual translations of portions of the Bible. Examples of these are New Testament translations by J. B. Phillips and C. B. Williams. There are other translations—too numerous to mention.

Read and familiarize yourself with various translations. This can be helpful not only for yourself but for others who are interested in Bible reading.

Determine the reading level and desires of the people involved. Consider something like *Today's English Version* for younger audiences or those learning English, while reserving the *New American Standard* and the *King James Version* for people with higher reading levels.

Determine the goal of a group's or individual's Bible study. Some may need a more literal *New American Standard*. A more literary *New Revised Standard Version* or *New International Version* may be more appropriate.

Consider the desire of the reader. Is traditional language, literal accuracy, literary quality, ease of reading, or simply affirmation of the current translation in use most important?

The Bible was written in the language of the people. As we have seen, dedicated scholars have sought to do the same through translations. At times these translations may vary in wording. But for the most part they do not vary in meaning. Any translation is interpretative in nature. The translator renders the Bible as he/she understands it. Nevertheless the old saying is true. It is not the parts of the Bible which I do not understand that bother me. It is that which I understand—but do not do.

I have a friend now retired, who for almost 50 years taught the Greek New Testament in two of our seminaries. He is as familiar with the Greek text as with any English version, even reading it in his daily devotions. The story is told that some years ago he was asked to serve as interim pastor of a church. For three straight Sundays he read his Scripture from the Greek New Testament—translating it, of course. After the third Sunday the deacons told him not to return, saying, "We want someone who preaches the Bible." All the while he was leading them to drink from the original "fountain"!

Not many can read the Bible in the original languages. But because many of our forebears paid so great a price, you can read it in your own language. So read it, believe it, and live by it. It is God's revealed and inspired word to you.

The Bible:

Its
Message
for Today

Chapter 10
The Bible: Its Message for Today

Thus far in this volume we have dealt largely with technical matters. Now we face the inevitable question: What does the Bible mean to me? Is it simply a collection of ancient writings, even legends and myths? Or, at best, is it historically accurate as it relates the spiritual experiences of the ancients, but has no relevant message for modern man? It met the needs of those who lived in a relatively simple age. But does it have a message for our complex Space Age?

In our journey through this little book we have noted that the Bible is true history. It does not claim to be a textbook in ancient history. Neither does it relate all of ancient history. It relates only that history which has a bearing upon God's redemptive purpose. In doing so it records history not found in other history books. It is history within history of God's *holy history* of His mighty acts within the arena of history.

While the Bible records definite events about real people, it is not confined to those particular periods and events. It declares eternal truth applicable to any people in a given time.

Jesus said, "Think not that I am come to destroy the law, or the prophets: I am not come to destroy, but to fulfill. For verily I say unto you, Till heaven and earth pass, one jot or one tittle shall in no wise pass from the law, till all be fulfilled" (Matt. 5:17-18). And Peter, quoting Isaiah 40:8, says, "The grass withereth, and the flower thereof falleth away: But the word of the Lord endureth for ever" (1 Pet. 1:24-25). For instance, the Ten Commandments are not true simply because they are in the Bible. They are in the Bible because they are eternally true. No person or people can live contrary to them without paying the price of such.

So the Bible does have a message for people today. This is true for many reasons.

God is still God. Often the Bible speaks of the righteous *fearing* God. It would read better as *reverencing* Him.

Someone has said that ours is a generation which has heroes. And for multitudes, God Himself is included among the neglected and ignored. A generation which bows before the altar of materialism has lost its sense of the sacred. The eternal, infinite God is not simply "the Man Upstairs."

Science moves from cause to effect. It can even move backward from material effect to material cause. But when it comes to basic matter it has gone as far as science can go. At that point religion must take over, as we take the leap of faith into the presence of the eternal God. Thus the Bible begins with "In the beginning God . . ." God is "Immanuel" (God with us, Matt. 1:23), but He is also "high and lifted up" (Isa. 6:1). The Bible teaches us that God is omnipresent (present simultaneously in all time and space), omniscient (all wise), and omnipotent (all powerful). But He is also holiness, righteousness, truth, and love.

Our age needs to read over and over the account of Jesus' transfiguration. The apostles had become so familiar with Him in flesh that they seem to have lost the concept of His deity so that they even argued with Him (Matt. 16:22). Matthew says that Jesus "began" to teach of His coming death and resurrection, and that Peter "began" to rebuke Him for it. This suggests that they began and continued to do this.

A week later Jesus took Peter, James, and John farther up Mt. Hermon. Luke 9:29 says that "as he (Jesus) prayed," He was transfigured. For what was Jesus praying? In light of what happened immediately thereafter, it seems that He was praying that the Father would give these apostles such a demonstration to remind them that He was more than a man with whom to argue; He was God in flesh to be obeyed.

Matthew 17:2 describes it thus. "His face did shine as the sun, and his rainment was white as the light." "As the sun" suggests brightness. But it suggests far more. It can mean that Jesus shone as the sun shines. It does not reflect the light of another body as does the moon. It shines out of the nature of its being. It was so with Jesus. It was the light of His deity shining forth so that the apostles saw Him as He really is— God of very God—in flesh.

We need to recapture such a vision of God as He really is in His triune being. We catch such a vision from the Bible.

Furthermore, we need the message of the Bible today because

Sin is still sin. Our morally corrupt world does not like that word. Philosophy calls it an upward stumbling in the progress of the human race. Psychology calls it maladjustment. Physiology calls it glandular disturbance. Sociology calls it bad environment. Ethics calls it the mores of the age. But God calls it *sin.*

When our primeval parents sinned they did not progress, they regressed. They were not afflicted with maladjustment or glandular disturbance. The mores of the age were toward righteousness. And the first sin was committed in a paradise.

One Greek word for sin means to miss the mark, like missing a target. The target is the holy, righteous nature of God. And "all (not some) have sinned, and come short of the glory of God" (Rom. 3:23). The penalty of sin is death (Rom. 6:23) or eternal separation from God.

Our age desperately needs a new concept of sin and its penalty. This comes only from the Bible.

Also we need the message of the Bible because *Man still needs redemption.* All of man's efforts to remedy his plight is like putting a bandaid on a cancer. Only the Bible gives the remedy for sin and lostness (Acts 4:12).

Redemption is the theme which runs throughout the Bible. Revelation 13:8 speaks of Christ as "the Lamb slain from the foundation of the world." Before God created the world or man, He knew that man would sin and need a Savior. So Christ was slain from before the foundation of the world. Forgiveness was in the heart of God before sin was in the heart of man.

But that which was a reality in eternity had to be wrought out in the arena of history in order that people might see and believe in the Redeemer for salvation. So God in Christ came into the world as a flesh and blood man—virgin-born, tempted in all points as we are, yet without sin—took our place as He died for our sins and was raised from the dead for our justification. Thus He proved that God was just in His demand for righteousness in us, and became the justifier of all who believe in Him (Rom. 3:26). Only in the Bible do we find this truth.

Furthermore, we need to read the Bible because

The missionary commission still stands. The Christian faith is a missionary faith. God sent His Son to redeem a lost world. And His Son sends His people to evangelize the world (Matt. 28:18-20; Luke 24:47-48; John 20:21; Acts 1:8).

The gospel was not entrusted to angels but to redeemed people. In Matthew 28 an angel rolled away the stone of Jesus' tomb, not to let Jesus out but to let the women in to see that the tomb was empty. He announced Jesus' resurrection and told the women to tell the apostles to meet Jesus in Galilee. Then he said, "Lo, I have told you" (v. 7).

These were His final words. In effect, God sent an angel to do what only an angel could do. Having finished His mission, He said that the rest of the work was left for redeemed people to do. In fact, Jesus founded His church for this very mission (Eph. 3:10-11).

The Bible is a missionary book from beginning to end.

In a southern city of the United States a deacon was invited to teach the Sunday School lesson for a men's class in a nearby church. The lesson was on missions. The deacon knew that the teacher of this class was antimissionary. So he made a list of missionary passages in the Bible and asked the teacher to read them without comment. After the teacher had read about three of these he stopped and commented. "I just swan fore goodness. The fudder you go, the worser it gits!" So it will be with anyone who seeks to oppose missions from the Bible.

We need to read the Bible because

Our inner needs are ever the same. Outward conditions of life may change: culture, modes of dress and travel, housing and the like. But people's inner needs are ever the same: a sense of lostness, loneliness, fear, worry and the like. And the ultimate answer to each of these is found in the Bible.

Many years ago a prominent European psychiatrist said that for 35 years, thousands of people had come to him with their personal problems. But he had never known one to solve his/her problem without first finding a right relationship with God. The Bible alone tells us how to do this.

William E. Gladstone has been quoted as saying, "If I am asked what is the remedy for the deeper sorrows of the human heart, I must point to something which in the well known hymn is called 'The old, old story,' told in an old, old Book and taught with the old, old teaching which is the greatest and best guide ever given to mankind."

We should read the Bible because

Its message is the preserver of nations. It tells of the fall of Israel and Judah because they forgot God.

Though the United States is still the greatest nation on earth, there are evidences of decay which should alarm us: staggering debt, environmental pollution, corruption in business and government, rampant crime, narcotics, illicit sex, broken homes—the list could be endless. The basic greatness of a nation is not its military might, political clout, or natural resources. It is the character of its people.

Daniel Webster has been quoted as prophetically saying, "If religious books are not widely circulated among the masses in this country, and the people do not become religious, I do not know what is to become of us as a nation. And the thought is one to cause solemn reflection on the part of every patriot and Christian. If truth be not diffused, error will be; if God and His Word are not known and received, the devil and his works will gain the ascendancy; if the evangelical volume does not reach every hamlet, the pages of a corrupt and licentious literature will; if the power of the gospel is not felt through the length and breadth of the land, anarchy and misrule, degradation and misery, corruption and darkness, will reign without mitigation or end."

The Bible should be read because

It gives hope in the present. Jesus said, "In this world ye shall have tribulation (be in a tight place with seemingly no way out): but be of good cheer (courage); I have overcome (fully conquered) the world" (John 16:33).

For emphasis recall a fact related earlier in this book. Revelation was written in the midst of religious persecution. Christians refused to worship the Roman emperor Domitian (A.D. 81-96). John himself was in exile on the isle of Patmos. On the mainland Christians were persecuted unmercifully; some even became martyrs for their faith.

We may well imagine that they were asking questions. Has God been dethroned? Is Satan on the throne of the universe? Does God know what is happening to us? Does He care? Worse still, does He know and care but is powerless to act on our behalf?

It was then that John was told not to look about at what is happening on earth but to look up and see what is happening in heaven (Rev. 4-5). Looking up he saw that a "throne was set in heaven, and one sat on the throne" (4:2). "Was set" means that there was never a time when that throne was not there. God was still on His throne! "A rainbow round about the throne" symbolizes God's protection of His people. And John saw a redeemed natural order or creation joined with redeemed people in heaven as they praised God for His creative work. In Revelation 5 he saw them praising Christ or the Lamb for His redemptive work. Curses on earth, but praises in heaven.

But the thing of present interest is a scroll sealed with seven seals or completely sealed. A strong angel asked, "Who is worthy to open the book, and to loose the seals thereof?" (5:2). This refers to revealing the contents of the scroll. "And no man in heaven, nor in earth, neither under the earth, was able to open the book, neither to look thereon" (5:3). Only the "Lamb as it had been slain" was worthy to do this.

Many ideas have been suggested as to the identity of this scroll. I see it as the scroll of history. To unseal it is to reveal its meaning. No man in heaven, or one still living on earth, or one in hell can give us the meaning of history. Only the slain Lamb can do so. The slain Lamb suggests God's redemptive work in Christ. In other words, the key to understanding history is God's redemptive purpose in Jesus Christ.

God is the God of history. He is not responsible for the evil deeds of men and nations. But in it all God is overruling the evil and is guiding history toward the accomplishment of His redemptive purpose. Only thus can we understand the true meaning of history. And that is the story contained in the Bible.

Finally, we should read the Bible because

It tells of the final victory of Christ. No matter how dark the moment may be, the ultimate goal of history is the triumph of God in Christ over all evil. This is the theme of Revelation. But it is also the theme of the Bible as a whole (Gen. 3:15). Isaiah 11 pictures the Messianic Age as one of peace and righteousness. Following His resurrection Jesus said that all authority in heaven and earth was His (Matt. 28:18). Paul pictures God—Father, Son, and Holy Spirit—as "all in all" in the universe (1 Cor. 15:28).

Revelation 11:15 reads, literally, "The sovereignties of the cosmos (universe) became that of our Lord and of his Christ; and he shall reign as sovereign unto the ages of the ages." "Unto the ages of the ages" is the strongest Greek phrase for eternity. "Became" expresses a point in history when this became a reality. In combination with Matthew 28:18, I see this happening when Jesus came forth from the tomb. But relate this to Revelation 19:16. Following the battle of Armageddon (Rev. 19:11-15) it is said of Christ that "he hath on his vesture and on his thigh a name written, KING OF KINGS, AND LORD OF LORDS" (v. 16).

The forces of evil may seem to run rampant throughout the earth. But in the words of another, we must learn what the centuries have to say against the hours. The message of the Bible is one of hope, yea, of assurance. *Those who trust in the Lord are on the winning side.* Therefore, the Bible has a message for us.

Just use me—I am the Bible.
I am God's wonderful library.
I am always—and above all—the Truth.
To the weary pilgrim, I am a good strong staff.
To the one who sits in the gloom, I am a glorious light.
To those who stoop beneath heavy burdens, I am sweet rest.
To him who has lost his way, I am a safe guide.
To those who have been hurt by sin, I am a healing balm.
To the discouraged, I whisper glad messages of hope.
To those who are distressed by the storms of life, I am an anchor.
To those who suffer in lonely solitude, I am a cool, soft hand resting on a fevered brow.
O, child of man, to best defend me, just use me!
*   —Anonymous*[1]

Footnotes

Chapter 2

1. A. T. Robertson, *Word Pictures in the New Testament, Vol. III* (Nashville: Broadman Press, 1930), 288.

2. T. C. Smith, "Acts," *The Broadman Bible Commentary, Vol. 10,* gen. ed. Clifton J. Allen (Nashville: Broadman Press, 1970), 104.

3. Ariel and Will Durant, *The Lessons of History* (New York: Simon and Schuster, 1968), 11.

4. Edward Allison McDowell, *The Meaning and Message of Revelation* (Nashville: Broadman Press, 1951).

5. Herschel H. Hobbs, *The Cosmic Drama* (Waco: Word Books, 1972), 77.

Chapter 3

1. M. K. Kyle, "Archaeology and Criticism," *The International Standard Bible Encyclopedia, Vol. I,* gen. ed. James Orr (Grand Rapids: Wm. B. Eerdmans Publishing Co., 1915), 227.

2. Jack Finegan, *Light From the Ancient Past, The Archaeological Background of Judaism and Christianity* (Princeton: Princeton University Press, 1959), vii.

3. *ISBE*, Vol. II, 749.

4. *Op. Cit.*, 749.

5. Finegan, *Op. Cit.*, 267-268.

6. Finegan, *Op. Cit.*, 268-269.

7. *Op. Cit.*, 277-278.

8. *Op. Cit.*, 352. See also A. T. Robertson, *Luke the Historian in the Light of Research* (New York: Charles Scribner's Sons, 1930), 195.

9. A. T. Robertson, *Op. Cit.*, 1.

10. *Op. Cit.*, 119.

11. Finegan, *Op. Cit.*, 258.

12. *Op. Cit.*, 259-260.

13. *Op. Cit.*, 260.

14. Robertson, *Op. Cit.*, 128.
15. *Op. Cit.*, 122.
16. *Op. Cit.*, 125.
17. Finegan, *Op. Cit.*, 229.
18. *Op. Cit.*, 321-322.

Chapter 4

1. Ronald E. Clements, "Leviticus," *The Broadman Bible Commentary, Vol. 2*, gen. ed. Clifton J. Allen (Nashville: Broadman Press, 1970), 1.

2. John Joseph Owens, "Numbers," *The Broadman Bible Commentary, Vol. 2* (Nashville: Broadman Press, 1970), 75.

3. *Ibid.*

4. *Op. Cit.*, 175.

Chapter 5

1. Ben F. Philbeck, Jr., "1-2 Samuel," *The Broadman Bible Commentary, Vol. 3*, gen. ed. Clifton J. Allen (Nashville: Broadman Press, 1970), 1.

2. Philbeck, *Op. Cit.*, 146.

3. *The Holy Bible* (Nashville: Holman Bible Publishers, 1982), "A Survey on Each Book of the Bible."

4. *Ibid.*

5. John D. W. Watts, "Zechariah," *The Broadman Bible Commentary, Vol. 7*, gen. ed. Clifton J. Allen (Nashville: Broadman Press, 1970), 308.

Chapter 6

1. Frank Stagg, *The Book of Acts* (Nashville: Broadman Press, 1955), 1-18.

Chapter 7

1. G. Campbell Morgan, D. D., *The Corinthian Letter of Paul* (New York: Fleming H. Revell Company, 1946), 19.

2. Gerhard Kittle, *Theological Dictionary of the New Testament, Vol. VI* (Grand Rapids: Wm. B. Eerdmans Publishing Co., 1968), 877-879.

Chapter 8

1. For a fuller discussion see articles by George L. Robinson and J. S. Riggs, *The International Standard Bible Encyclopedia, Vol. I,* gen. ed. James Orr (Grand Rapids: Wm. B. Eerdmans Publishing Co., 1915), 554-566. This author is greatly in debt to these articles.

2. *Op. Cit.*, 555.

3. *Ibid.*

4. *Op. Cit.*, 565.

Chapter 10

1. Virginia Ely, *I Quote* (New York: George W. Stewart Publishing, Inc., 1947), 33-34.

Personal Learning Activities

Chapter 1
1. From what two Greek words does our word "Bible" come? What do they mean?
2. The Bible is composed of how many books? How many authors were involved? Over what period of time were the books written?
3. Define the following terms: revelation, progressive revelation, inspiration, verbal plenary theory, dynamic theory, and illumination.

Chapter 2
1. Why is it important to understand the historical context related to persons and events in the Bible?
2. How do Acts 17:25-28, 1 Corinthians 15:25-28, and Romans 8:28 help us discover the divine philosophy of history?
3. What is meant by "redemption history"?

Chapter 3
1. Define "archaeology" and explain how it helps us understand Bible terms.
2. Identify the two principle methods of Bible study referred to by the term "biblical criticism," and define each.
3. Give one illustration of how each of the following archaeological finds has contributed to our understanding of the Scriptures and their authenticity: papyri, Dead Sea Scrolls, and inscriptions.

Chapter 4
1. What is the meaning of "testament" and Pentateuch?
2. How did the covenant in Exodus 19 differ from the covenant with Abraham in Genesis?

3. With what subject does Leviticus deal?
4. What passage in Deuteronomy summarizes the whole book?

Chapter 5
1. Give a brief outline of Judges.
2. What are the terms of Ezra and Nehemiah?
3. What ancient idea is refuted in Job?
4. List the Major Prophets and Minor Prophets.

Chapter 6
1. What is meant by the interbiblical period?
2. What does "synoptic" mean? List the synoptic gospels.
3. What is the purpose of John's gospel? What is the format of the book?
4. Who is the author of Acts?

Chapter 7
1. Which of Paul's epistles is a circular letter to the churches of Asia?
2. What is the keynote of Philippians?
3. List the pastoral epistles.
4. What is the overriding theme of Revelation?

Chapter 8
1. Define "canon" in its basic meaning and current usage.
2. What three human factors were important as the Holy Spirit guided in forming the canon of the Scriptures?
3. What are the date and decision of the Council of Carthage?
4. Was the decision about the canon of Scripture from the grass roots up or was it handed down by councils?

Chapter 9
1. In what languages were most of the Old Testament and New Testament written?
2. Who made the first complete translation of the Bible from Latin into English?
3. Who was the first translator of the Greek New Testament into English?
4. List 4 of the major English translations and give their publication dates.

Chapter 10
1. Give 5 reasons why the Bible has a message for people today.
2. Write a statement about what the Bible means to you personally.
3. According to the last line of the chapter, how can we best defend the Bible?

The Church Study Course

The Church Study Course is a Southern Baptist education system designed to support the training efforts of local churches. It provides courses, recognition, record keeping and regular reports from some 20,000 participating churches.

The Church Study Course is characterized by short courses ranging from 2½ to 10 hours in length. They may be studied individually or in groups. With more than 600 courses in 24 subject areas, it offers 130 diploma plans in all areas of church leadership and Christian growth. Diplomas represent hours of study, knowledge and skills acquired, and approval of the sponsoring agency.

While the heart of the Church Study Course is leadership training, many courses are available for all members. Each year, approximately 900,000 awards and 170,000 diplomas are earned by adults and youth. While youth may receive credit on any of the courses, some courses are designed especially for youth. Also available in the system are non-credit short courses for children and preschoolers.

Originating in 1902 with two Sunday School courses, the Church Study Course now serves all church programs and is jointly sponsored by many agencies within the Southern Baptist Convention. Sponsors include: Baptist Sunday School Board, Woman's Missionary Union, Brotherhood Commission, Home Mission Board, Foreign Mission Board, Stewardship Commission, Education Commission, and the respective departments of the state conventions and associations affiliated with the Southern Baptist Convention.

Records are kept by the Sunday School Board for the other agencies. A state-of-the-art computer system maintains records for more than one million individual students and provides regular reports to participating churches. After enrollment in a diploma plan(s), diplomas are issued automatically as requirements are met. Credit earned in one church is recognized in all other Southern Baptist churches.

Complete details about the Church Study Course system, courses available, and diplomas offered may be found in a current copy of the *Church Study Course Catalog*.

How to Request Credit for this Course

This book is the text for course number 04-125 in the subject area: "Bible Studies." This course is designed for 5 hours of group study.

Credit for this course may be obtained in two ways:
1. Read the book and attend class sessions. (If you are absent from one or more sessions, complete the "Personal Learning Activities" for the material missed.)
2. Read the book and complete the "Personal Learning Activities." (Written work should be submitted to an appropriate church leader.)

A request for credit may be made on Form 725 "Church Study Course Enrollment/Credit Request" and sent to the Awards Office, Sunday School Board, 127 Ninth Avenue, North, Nashville, Tennessee 37234. The form on the following page may be used to request credit. Enrollment in a diploma may also be made on Form 725.

Within three months of your completion of a course, confirmation of your credit will be sent to your church. A copy of your complete transcript will be sent to your church annually during the July—September quarter if you have completed a course during the previous 12 months.

CHURCH STUDY COURSE ENROLLMENT/CREDIT REQUEST

FORM - 725 (Rev. 1-89)

MAIL THIS REQUEST TO ➡

CHURCH STUDY COURSE AWARDS OFFICE
BAPTIST SUNDAY SCHOOL BOARD
127 NINTH AVENUE, NORTH
NASHVILLE, TENNESSEE 37234

Is this the first course taken since 1983? ☐ YES If yes, or not sure complete all of Section 1. ☐ NO If no, complete only bold boxes in Section 1.

SECTION 1 - STUDENT I.D.

Social Security Number

☐ Mr. ☐ Miss
☐ Mrs.

Personal CSC Number * ➡

DATE OF BIRTH

Month	Day	Year

STUDENT

Name (First, MI, Last)

Street, Route, or P.O. Box

City, State — Zip Code

CHURCH

Church Name

Mailing Address

City, State — Zip Code

SECTION 3 - COURSE CREDIT REQUEST

Course No.	Title (use exact title)
1. 04-125	Getting Acquainted with the Bible
2.	
3.	
4.	
5.	
6.	

SECTION 4 - DIPLOMA ENROLLMENT

Enter exact diploma title from current Church Study Course catalog. Indicate diploma age group if appropriate. Do not enroll again with each course. When all requirements have been met, the diploma will be mailed to your church. Enrollment in Christian Development Diplomas is automatic. No charge will be made for enrollment or diplomas.

Title of Diploma	Age group or area
Title of Diploma	Age group or area
Signature of Pastor, Teacher, or Other Church Leader	Date

SECTION 2 - CHANGE REQUEST ONLY (Current inf. in Section 1)

☐ Former Name

☐ Former Address — Zip Code

☐ Former Church — Zip Code

*CSC # not required for new students. Others please give CSC # when using SS # for the first time. Then, only one ID # is required.